Antisemitism: A Very Short Introduction

VERY SHORT INTRODUCTIONS are for anyone wanting a stimulating and accessible way in to a new subject. They are written by experts, and have been published in more than 25 languages worldwide.

The series began in 1995, and now represents a wide variety of topics in history, philosophy, religion, science, and the humanities. Over the next few years it will grow to a library of around 200 volumes – a Very Short Introduction to everything from ancient Egypt and Indian philosophy to conceptual art and cosmology.

Very Short Introductions available now:

AFRICAN HISTORY
    John Parker and Richard Rathbone
AMERICAN POLITICAL
    PARTIES AND
    ELECTIONS L. Sandy Maisel
THE AMERICAN
    PRESIDENCY Charles O. Jones
ANARCHISM Colin Ward
ANCIENT EGYPT Ian Shaw
ANCIENT PHILOSOPHY
    Julia Annas
ANCIENT WARFARE
    Harry Sidebottom
ANGLICANISM Mark Chapman
THE ANGLO-SAXON AGE
    John Blair
ANIMAL RIGHTS David DeGrazia
ANTISEMITISM Steven Beller
ARCHAEOLOGY Paul Bahn
ARCHITECTURE
    Andrew Ballantyne
ARISTOTLE Jonathan Barnes
ART HISTORY Dana Arnold
ART THEORY Cynthia Freeland

THE HISTORY OF
    ASTRONOMY Michael Hoskin
ATHEISM Julian Baggini
AUGUSTINE Henry Chadwick
BARTHES Jonathan Culler
BESTSELLERS John Sutherland
THE BIBLE John Riches
THE BRAIN Michael O'Shea
BRITISH POLITICS
    Anthony Wright
BUDDHA Michael Carrithers
BUDDHISM Damien Keown
BUDDHIST ETHICS
    Damien Keown
CAPITALISM James Fulcher
THE CELTS Barry Cunliffe
CHAOS Leonard Smith
CHOICE THEORY
    Michael Allingham
CHRISTIAN ART
    Beth Williamson
CHRISTIANITY Linda Woodhead
CLASSICS Mary Beard and
    John Henderson

Available soon:

For more information visit our web site

www.oup.co.uk/general/vsi/

Steven Beller

ANTISEMITISM

A Very Short Introduction

OXFORD
UNIVERSITY PRESS

OXFORD

UNIVERSITY PRESS

Great Clarendon Street, Oxford ox2 6dp

Oxford University Press is a department of the University of Oxford.
It furthers the University's objective of excellence in research, scholarship,
and education by publishing worldwide in

Oxford New York

Auckland Cape Town Dar es Salaam Hong Kong Karachi
Kuala Lumpur Madrid Melbourne Mexico City Nairobi
New Delhi Shanghai Taipei Toronto

With offices in

Argentina Austria Brazil Chile Czech Republic France Greece
Guatemala Hungary Italy Japan Poland Portugal Singapore
South Korea Switzerland Thailand Turkey Ukraine Vietnam

Oxford is a registered trade mark of Oxford University Press
in the UK and in certain other countries

Published in the United States
by Oxford University Press Inc., New York

© Steven Beller 2007

British Library Cataloguing in Publication Data

Data available

Library of Congress Cataloging in Publication Data

Data available

ISBN 978–0–19–289277–5

1 3 5 7 9 10 8 6 4 2

Typeset by SPI Publisher Services, Pondicherry, India
Printed in Great Britain
on acid-free paper by
Ashford Colour Press Ltd, Gosport, Hampshire

Contents

Contents

Acknowledgements

Writing a Very Short Introduction to any subject has its problems and challenges, but I suspect writing one on such a sensitive and unfortunately all too relevant topic as antisemitism is just asking for trouble. To what extent I have avoided this, while still adding some light to an emotion-laden and indeed horror-filled subject, I leave to the reader's judgement. That I attempted it at all is partly due to a suggestion by Christopher Clark, whom I nevertheless thank. An anonymous reader and David Sorkin offered me generous and invaluable advice on avoiding some major pitfalls, and I am most grateful to both. Whether I succeeded in avoiding those pitfalls is, however, something I alone can answer for.

Over the course of writing this book, I also learned a great deal from the many related discussions on the Humanities Net's h-antisemitism, and am thankful for the opportunity to hone some of my ideas in that forum. The University of Cambridge; University College, London; American University; Georgetown University; the Institute for Advanced Study in Princeton; George Washington University; the Institute for the Human Sciences and the International Research Centre for Cultural Studies, both in Vienna, also provided the opportunity to learn with students and exchange views with colleagues, from all of which I very much benefited. To the many colleagues and friends in other academic and non-academic settings in Britain, America, Europe, Israel, and elsewhere who have helped and stimulated me to think on this topic, I also give thanks. I trust they will understand if here I thank just two representative of all: Ivar Oxaal and Peter Pulzer.

I would further like to thank Oxford University Press for allowing me to write this book in the VSI series, and for their great patience in seeing the project through, especially George Miller, Marsha Filion, and, in the end, Luciana O'Flaherty and James Thompson. I would also like to thank Zoë Spilberg for her diligence and persistence in arranging for the illustrations for the book; and Alyson Silverwood for copy-editing.

To my parents, Milton and Hermi Beller, I owe the opportunity to be able to write this book in the first place, and not a little, I suspect, of the motivation to do so. To my most generous parents-in-law, Andrew and Doris Brimmer, I also wish to express my deepest gratitude for their multi-faceted support. To their daughter, my wife, Esther Diane Brimmer, I owe as much as a man is able. To her, above all, I owe the existence of my son, Nathaniel Alexander Brimmer-Beller. It is to him and the memory of his grandfather, Milton Beller, that this book is dedicated – in the hope that the world my son inherits is one in which the subject of this book, so much a part of my father's world, is but a distant and painful lesson of a former time. We can but hope: there is always next year.

Steven Beller, Washington DC, at Passover, 2007

List of illustrations

The publisher and the author apologize for any errors or omissions in the above list. If contacted they will be pleased to rectify these at the earliest opportunity.

Chapter 1
What is antisemitism?

Antisemitism is a hatred of Jews that has stretched across millennia and across continents; or it is a relatively modern political movement and ideology that arose in Central Europe in the late 19th century and achieved its evil apogee in the Holocaust; or it is the irrational, psychologically pathological version of an ethnocentric and religiocentric anti-Judaism that originated in Christianity's conflict with its Jewish roots – and achieved its evil apogee in the Holocaust; or it is a combination of all of these. It all depends on how one defines the term. This book will focus on the political movement and ideology: how it came about, how its ideological claims became integrated into European and Western political, but also social, intellectual, and cultural, life, and how the particular Central European context enabled it to lead into the Holocaust.

Some concepts, such as communism, while complicated to explain, are fairly simple to define and identify as an ideology and political movement, and just that. Antisemitism, in contrast, is a highly ambivalent, even multivalent term, which can cause great confusion. As with communism, it is definable as a self-styled ideology and political movement, set up in 1879 by Wilhelm Marr, as the 'Antisemites League', to combat 'Semitism' (hence the often used, but ill-advised, orthography of 'anti-Semitism'). Yet it is also often understood as a psychological category, ranging from mild pejorative prejudice against Jews as different to the full-blown pathology of an exterminationist, paranoid hatred of Jews as a race out to destroy Western (Aryan) civilization; and this psychological understanding of antisemitism has led to the latter being seen as a deep-seated pathology not only within the psyches of individual inhabitants of the West, but of the collective 'discourse' of Western civilization, and even 'modernity', generally.

The study of antisemitism has also, of necessity, been dominated by the role it played in causing the worst case of genocide in modern history: the extermination of European Jewry that has come to be known as the Holocaust or the Shoah. So powerful has the Holocaust been in shaping our understanding of antisemitism that many people define antisemitism in terms of its causation of that genocide – in a form of 'Whig history' in reverse. Partly as a result, leading authorities in the field such as Bernard Lewis have come to define antisemitism as *only* the irrational thinking that derives from the Christian relationship to Judaism; Gavin Langmuir has gone further, coining the term 'chimeric' to describe the completely irrational, delusional thinking that could make people believe that Jews, as a race, were so evil that they had to be exterminated, regardless of the empirical evidence to the contrary. The problem with this definition is that there were many individual, self-styled 'antisemites' who were shocked and horrified at the murderous excess of the 'Final Solution', just as in the period before the First World War there were many politicians who campaigned as 'antisemites' but whose demands regarding Jews extended to not much more than mundane discrimination, and who rejected the extremism of others. Similarly, as I shall argue, the developments that led to the Holocaust involved a large degree of instrumental rationality that only remotely relied on 'irrational' illusions about Jews. Antisemitism and the Holocaust, though obviously closely connected, are not identical. Furthermore, antisemitism, if we are to make any sense of the term to describe the political movement of the late 19th and 20th centuries, cannot be confined to the psychologically pathological realm of the irrational.

I intend to make clear that this political and ideological movement could not have arisen without the context of the psychological form of antisemitism which, for the sake of clarity, I shall call 'Jew-hatred'. Yet the latter will not be the main focus of my discussion of 'antisemitism', nor will this ideational, psychological context be the sole context in which I discuss the political movement. Equally significant for the development and 'success' of antisemitism was the concrete historical context in which it existed, and the specific historical events and sets of circumstances which 'antisemites' experienced. A most significant factor in this historical context was the presence and behaviour of European (and later American) Jews.

It might seem redundant to claim that actual Jews have a place in a study of antisemitism, were it not for the fact that recent developments in the historiography of antisemitism have tended to minimize and marginalize, even dispute any significance at all for, the part played by Jews as the target and foil for antisemitism. The better histories of modern antisemitism, such as Jakob Katz's *From Prejudice to Destruction* and Peter Pulzer's *The Rise of Political Antisemitism in Germany and Austria*, usually do acknowledge the significance of the actual Jewish population in the complex dialectic of the development of antisemitism. Yet much of recent academic discussion of antisemitism has virtually excluded the Jewish aspect from consideration.

One very understandable reason for this has been the wish to avoid even the appearance of making Jews in any way responsible, let alone 'guilty', for an enmity which led to genocide against them. Even a very mild (if poorly articulated) form of such an assertion in Albert Lindemann's history of antisemitism, *Esau's Tears*, was met with outrage by prominent scholars in the field such as Robert

3

Wistrich. Misplaced as I think it was in that instance, the outrage nevertheless has a point. As Jean-Paul Sartre famously pointed out many decades ago, antisemitism is not a *Jewish* problem, it is a problem for *non-Jews*, and must primarily be viewed and understood as such, as 'our (non-Jews') fault'. Hence the causes of it, and the responsibility for it, must be sought among non-Jews, not blamed on Jews. This is all well and good, but when taken too literally it results in a strange self-contained world in which Jews become a caricature of passive victimhood that quite belies their extraordinary participation in modern world culture, thought and history. Protected in the schema of studies of antisemitism from having any responsible role in antisemitism's causation, Jews are as a result also denied any *positive* responsibility in Western history, thus ironically perpetuating one of the original sources of antisemitic prejudice, the idea that Jews are 'outside of history'.

The main problem with much of contemporary discussion of antisemitism, following the lead of postmodernist literary criticism, is that it occurs on a merely discursive level, as though it bore no relation at all to the realities of Jewish existence in the late 19th and early 20th centuries. This effectively prohibits looking at how Jews actually interacted with non-Jewish society, because the development of antisemitism as a 'discourse' is held to be independent of the social, economic, and political reality. This claim of autonomy is inherent to the strategy of the proponents of the discursive methodology, such as Sander Gilman, but in the study of antisemitism it has oddly solipsistic results.

If antisemitic discourse can be studied independently of the target of its allegations, and if it was deeply lodged in the dominant discourse of Western civilization, then, it follows, it is the antisemites' view of Jews that is significant, not how actual Jews were. Moreover, following this logic, because the antisemitic discourse was dominant, empirical Jews were not only irrelevant to the antisemitic discourse, but were effectively influenced, shaped, and hence 'created', by it. Individuals of Jewish descent

4

growing up in this antisemitically informed discourse supposedly internalized the antisemitic image of the Jew, becoming to some degree 'Jewish self-haters', whose damaged, distorted psyches then affirmed the antisemitic Jewish stereotype. Just as the 'anti-Judaism' of the medieval Church became a self-fulfilling prophecy in denigrating and oppressing Jews to such an extent that they came to appear worthy of denigration and oppression, so, according to students of modern antisemitism, antisemites, in their discrimination against and rejection of modern Jews, created a self-fulfilling prophecy, driving Jews to an 'inauthenticity' and self-denial that confirmed antisemitic preconceptions. Modern Jewish history from this perspective, Holocaust or not, is largely the product of antisemitism.

The ill effects of this concentration at the discursive level concerning antisemitism have been compounded by a tendency, ironically perhaps, to discuss antisemitism with a discourse laden with metaphors of disease. This partially stems, no doubt, from the sense of antisemitism's irrationality. Hence antisemitic ideology and discourse are seen as inherently and pathologically irrational, a mental 'disease' that had infected the core of Western civilization, and that, while endemic for centuries, reached epidemic proportions and then pandemic proportions in the 1930s and 1940s, as the 'madness' of genocidal antisemitism spread like a 'virus' over so much of Europe. Some such metaphors might originally have had a valid purpose, especially for describing the more irrational aspects of antisemitic ideology, yet, as the previous sentence illustrates, metaphors of mental disease all too easily become conflated in current descriptions of antisemitism with metaphors of disease generally, reifying its subject as something with a will of its own, a contagious 'virus', beyond the capacity of any individual to control or combat.

This nosological approach to antisemitism is problematic for at least two reasons. First, it eerily repeats the same use of metaphors of disease by antisemites to describe the Jewish menace, whether it be the Jew as parasite, the Jew as genetic degenerate, or the 'virus' of Judaeo-Bolshevism, or the need to exterminate Jews as vermin, or bacilli. Second, by suggesting that antisemitism is a disease, and as such an irrational force of nature, it suggests that the individual antisemites who discriminated against, persecuted, and murdered Jews were themselves 'infected' by something, an ideology or a delusion, beyond their power, and hence not really morally responsible for their actions. If antisemitism is a 'disease', the product of the 'diseased' discourse of Western civilization, then antisemitic perpetrators were not responsible for their actions, the discourse that led them to do it is to blame. Antisemites become victims rather than perpetrators. This obscures the instrumental rationality often implicated in antisemitism and the moral culpability of those involved.

A related, partly countervailing development in the study of antisemitism has been to regard it and its genocidal result in the Holocaust as a product of 'modernity'. This critique, following another postmodernist approach pioneered by Zygmunt Bauman, neatly reverses the usual assumption that antisemitism and the Holocaust were an atavistic, 'irrational' rejection of modernity, the result of a horrific survival of medieval superstition and prejudice in an era of progress and spreading enlightenment and modernization. Instead, it is seen as a product of social and economic modernization, and the rationalization of complex ethnic and social contexts. This insight of antisemitism as a *modern* phenomenon has quite a long pedigree, going back at least to the Zionist ideology of Theodor Herzl, and, as we shall see, it contains more truth than might at first be evident. It at least raises the consideration that there were many rationalistic aspects to antisemitic thought, that antisemites often regarded themselves as participating in a 'scientific discourse', and that there were 'modern' instrumental rationalities to antisemitic practice and policy, including the industrialization of mass murder in the Holocaust.

The problem with this linkage of antisemitism and the Holocaust with modernity is that in most instances it conflates too easily the various forms of modernity and hence draws over-generalized conclusions about a 'modernity' based on only one specific German/Central European form. Responsibility for antisemitism and the Holocaust is attributed too generously and hence inaccurately. While emphasizing the 'rational' over the 'irrational' in the career of antisemitism, this assigning of the blame for antisemitism on 'modernity' ends up coming to a similar conclusion as the 'diseased' discourse of Western civilization approach: not the antisemites themselves, but modernity and Western civilization, are to blame for antisemitism's monstrous result; not the perpetrators, but all of us, are guilty.

As will have become evident, I do not think that looking at antisemitism only on the discursive level works; I think using the metaphor of disease to describe antisemitism's career is perniciously deceptive; and linking antisemitism with modernity, while leading to important insights, needs to be treated carefully and narrowly if it is to yield accurate conclusions. I do not accept the claim that European Jews were the creatures of Christian Europe; despite their oppression over centuries, European Jewry, both Sephardic and Ashkenazi, retained their own culture and intellectual heritage, and remained an independent factor in European society and hence history, and this became even more so in the modern era. Conversely, the individuals who joined the antisemitic movement, took part in the discrimination against and persecution of Jews, and benefited from this, were not only victims of their cultural heritage, but rather made conscious, rational, if highly immoral, choices from within that heritage, which were influenced by the actual condition and behaviour of actual Jews. That this heritage differed from that of other parts of the Western, 'modern' world nevertheless played a crucial role in enabling antisemites to succeed within societies that were not themselves inherently, or inevitably, antisemitic.

In a Very Short Introduction only the outlines of this complex phenomenon can be traced. Although a narrative approach is a necessary part of explaining the dynamic of the movement of antisemitism, such narratives are provided in several reliable standard works on the subject. What this book attempts is to outline the components of the phenomenon of antisemitism, and the key, tragic interactions between these components that led to the Holocaust. One of these interactions was between the cultural and intellectual assumptions of European society and the social and economic realities of modernization; another, closely related interaction was between what Europeans believed about Jews and the reality of Jewish existence in Europe. That these interactions came to a head in German Central Europe was not accidental. Understanding the reasons why this was, and why the Holocaust did not take place elsewhere, will help us to understand antisemitism, and also suggest some lessons for us about combating antisemitism and other forms of prejudice in the present and the future.

1. 'Synagogue', Strasbourg Cathedral (c. 1230). A common part of medieval Christian iconography, the depiction of Judaism as a blind woman was intended to symbolize the benighted nature of the Jewish refusal to recognize the truth of Christianity.

Chapter 2
The burden of the past

The emergence and success of antisemitism in the late 19th and 20th centuries cannot be understood without recognition of the large part played by a centuries-long heritage of Christian doctrinal hostility to Jews. This 'anti-Judaism' was an inherent part of Christianity after Paul, and was virtually inevitable once Jews had rejected the essential Christian claim that Jesus of Nazareth was the Christ. This conflict over beliefs led to the institutionalization within medieval European Christendom of the Jews as a protected, but oppressed minority. Doctrinally, Jews, cast in Christian theology as 'Christ's killers', were to be held in a subordinate and wretched state in order to act as evidence of the consequences of their blindness toward the truth of Christ's divinity, but this also meant that they were to be preserved, so that they could eventually act as witnesses, at the Second Coming, to that truth. As such, Jews were the sole minority faith tolerated within the confines of Western Christendom; and Jews also clearly played a *central* role, as the original Chosen People of the one God, to Christian understanding of the world.

This peculiar, negative eminence within the medieval Christian world view had perverse consequences for Jews and the image of Jews. The sophistication of the Church's doctrinal argument for protecting Jews was often cast to one side by radical popular movements and secular princes within Christendom. While there

Hildegardis

Gracianus

Petrus lombardus

Petrus comestor

Guilhelmus puer crucifixus

2. 'William of Norwich', print from the Nuremberg Chronicle (15th century). Found dead in 1144, 'Saint William', a tanner's apprentice, was the subject of the first allegation of Jewish ritual murder of a Christian child.

were episodes of persecution of Jews before the 11th century, and a severe limitation of their economic opportunities, the first major outburst of popular Jew-hatred came in northwestern Europe in the wake of the First Crusade in 1096, as mobs murdered Jews as 'Christ's killers'.

This hatred then took ever more irrational, delusionary forms, so that by the mid-12th century Jews came to be accused of the ritual murder of Christian children, the first such accusation coming over the death of William of Norwich in 1144. By the mid-13th century this had developed into the 'blood libel' whereby Jews were accused of draining Christian children of their blood in order to use it to bake matzos for Passover. Clerical and secular authorities occasionally pointed out the fabricated nature of such accusations, but at other times tacitly accepted them, the 'victims' of ritual murder becoming saints in the Catholic Church.

At the same time, the increasing restrictions on occupations open to Jews led to a concentration of Jews on the one occupation of moneylending (the taking of usury being theoretically proscribed for Christians). Their exposed social position, coupled with their expertise, also made them attractive to feudal rulers as a controllable source of royal financing and, with special taxes, revenue. Viewed functionally in terms of money, Jews became identified with money, even though most credit in the medieval economy was still provided by Christians, whether by individuals or institutions such as monasteries.

The situation, and the negative stereotype, of Jews worsened in the course of the Middle Ages. Forced to wear distinctive clothing by the Fourth Lateran Council in 1215, Jews were accused of desecrating the Host and poisoning wells, and were denigrated in such hideous iconography as the *Judensau* (Jewish pig) as no better than animals. They were also frequently the scapegoats when the Black Death decimated Europe in the mid-14th century. Their continued role as creditors, especially of rulers, merely made them more the target of popular resentment, and Jews were usually defenceless if their princely clients should decide that their persecution, banishment, or even execution were preferable to paying back debts. The result of this combination of popular prejudice and financial and political expediency was that Jews, despite official Church doctrine protecting their status, were expelled from England in 1290, France in 1394, much of Germany by 1350, from Spain in 1492, and Portugal in 1497. Orthodox Russia, before its imperial expansion in the 18th century, also prided itself on being free of Jews.

The 16th and 17th centuries saw renewed persecution and an elaboration of the Jewish negative stereotype. Martin Luther, after an initially positive attitude to Jews, turned against them when they rejected his demands to convert to the (his) true faith, and bequeathed a Jew-hating heritage to Lutheranism. Counter-Reformation Catholicism's general intolerance also extended to Jews, leading to the expulsion of Jews from Vienna in 1670. The re-emergence of the court Jew as financier to emperors, kings, and princes added to the stereotype of the Jew as the moneyman. The archetypal Jewish figure in early modern European popular culture was Shylock, a Jewish moneylender who demands his Christian 'pound of flesh'. The European conquest and colonizing of much of the rest of the world in the early modern era spread with it this negative Jewish stereotype, which therefore became virtually ubiquitous.

Anti-Jewish prejudice continued to receive institutional reinforcement into the 18th century. Andreas of Rinn, a Tyrolean ritual murder 'victim', was beatified in 1755; Maria Theresa attempted to expel the Jews from Prague in 1744. Outbursts of popular Jew-hatred continued in various parts of Europe into the 19th century, as evidenced by the Hep-Hep riots of 1819 in Germany. The negative Jewish stereotype, developed over centuries, clearly also survived in 19th-century European culture, in figures such as that other archetype of English literature, Fagin.

Even cases of ritual murder accusations persisted, for instance in Damascus in 1840, and Tiszaeszlar in 1882. The latter case was the occasion for one of the first campaigns of modern antisemitism. Modern antisemitism could not have occurred without this Christian-based heritage of Jew-hatred.

If anti-Jewish prejudice was a necessary condition of antisemitism's success, it was not, however, a sufficient one. It was not by any means constant: what Salo Baron called the 'lachrymose version of Jewish history' outlined above, of constant oppression and persecution, is deceptive in as much as it omits counter-developments and attitudes that by the 19th century had given many European Jews a much more positive and optimistic outlook on their future within European societies.

While Jews had been expelled from most of Western Europe by 1500, they had found refuge, and a degree of prosperity, in lands such as the Netherlands, northern Italy, and the Ottoman Empire. They had been welcomed *en masse* in Poland from the 13th century onwards, specifically to act as a commercial middle class between the landed nobility and the peasantry. For several centuries, Jews in Poland enjoyed relative tolerance and prosperity, and the Polish-Lithuanian Commonwealth was home to most of Ashkenazi Jewry into the 18th century.

Moreover, European history appeared to show that attitudes to Jews were quite capable of benevolent *change*. Perhaps the most spectacular transformation occurred in England, where Jews first returned in 1656; by the 18th century, the English political establishment, influenced partly by a theological philosemitism, was quite tolerant of Jews, even pro-Jewish. While there was some popular anti-Jewish sentiment, as evidenced by the protests against the Jew Bill of 1753, Jews were increasingly accepted as a part of English society. Benjamin Disraeli's achievement in becoming prime minister in 1874 was seen by many as a sign of British enlightenment concerning Jews. Disraeli was admittedly baptized as a child, and could not have reached his position had he not been, but the election of the first Jewish Lord Mayor of London in 1855, and the admittance of the first Jewish Member of Parliament in 1858 and first Member of the House of Lords in 1884 (both Rothschilds), allowed British public opinion by the late 19th century to pride itself on its positive attitude to Jews. Adolf Stöcker's attempts in the 1880s to spread the antisemitic message to England's shores were hence met with outraged incomprehension.

By the late 19th century, most of continental Europe had enacted full Jewish emancipation, and Western and Central European public opinion regarded the failure of those countries that had not done so, such as Tsarist Russia, as evidence of backwardness. Romanian resistance to granting its Jewish population equal rights made that country contemptible in Western opinion. Anti-Jewish sentiment clearly survived in much of Western and Central European society, but it was countered by a sense, derived from the Enlightenment and subsequent liberalism, that a modern society should tolerate people of other faiths. Even the continued anti-Judaism of the Roman Catholic Church could work in favour of Jews with public opinion, where a liberal, secular, anti-clerical culture had come to predominate in much of Western and Central Europe. In countries such as the Netherlands and Italy, Jews were accepted unproblematically as full members of society, nation, and state. In France, still torn between traditional Catholic-monarchist and revolutionary republican self-definitions, the situation was more complex, but the republican definition of national identity through citizenship, regardless of faith or ethnic background, allowed Jews to identity completely with the nation state.

In Central Europe, the birthplace of modern antisemitism, the situation was obviously less favourable to pro-Jewish attitudes. Parts of Germany so embraced the antisemitic message that they returned antisemitic deputies to the German parliament, and 19th-century German high culture was deeply influenced by the tradition of Jew-hatred, especially its high priest, Richard Wagner, who was truly antisemitic *avant la lettre*. The prevalence of ethnonationalist thinking among Germans, but also among Czech and Polish nationalists, also allowed Jew-hatred to facilitate the growth of antisemitism. The two 'capitals' of central Europe, Berlin and Vienna, had central roles in the career of political antisemitism, Berlin being the forcing ground of Stöcker's antisemitic Christian Socialism, and Vienna becoming the site of the greatest achievement of political antisemitism before 1914, Christian Social domination of the city's municipal government from 1895 on.

Even in Central Europe, however, there were crucial instances which show that anti-Jewish prejudice did not inevitably succeed in producing antisemitic political and sociocultural hegemony. In many parts of Germany, for instance, Jews continued to be prominent in local politics even when they were no longer so prominent on the national stage. In cities such as Breslau, and above all in Berlin, the particular array of political and social forces and the resulting continuing success of liberal political parties meant that Jews could feel almost as integrated into their social settings as their counterparts to the west. The record in the Habsburg Monarchy was similar. In Prague, Czech nationalist politicians were, it is true, not shy in exploiting anti-Jewish superstition and sentiment to further their cause. The Czech radical, Karel Baxa, who later became Prague's mayor, was a leading instigator of the Polna Affair of 1899–1900. In this miscarriage of justice, Leopold Hilsner was accused in collaboration with others of murder of a Christian girl, in other words ritual murder, and found guilty by a Czech jury. Yet, as Gary Cohen has well illustrated, the Czechs' German opponents in the national battle over Prague adopted the reverse tactic, of cooperating with and welcoming the support of Prague's German-speaking Jews.

It can well be argued that in the circumstances the Germans had little choice: Prague, which had at one point been regarded as a

'German' city, was by the late 19th century becoming ever more a Czech-speaking metropolis, as waves of Czechs came to the city from the surrounding, Czech-dominated countryside, and ethnic Czechs (and some Germans) opted for a Czech national identity over a German one, given increasing Czech predominance. The only group that remained as an ally to the German political establishment in the city in the struggle for German 'ethnic survival' was the relatively large Jewish community. The composition of that community was also becoming more Czech, as Czech-speaking Jews from the provincial towns and villages immigrated, and as formerly 'German' Jews became Czech due to political and economic pressure exerted by Czech nationalists. Yet a large number of Prague Jews retained a German national identity, and even more retained an allegiance to German culture, sending their children to German-speaking schools. This was the case with the 'Czech' parents of Franz Kafka, who nevertheless sent their son to a German school.

Faced with an anti-German and antisemitic Czech nationalist movement, German politicians and German-speaking Jews in Prague found themselves in alliance, even as German nationalists in the rest of German Bohemia became increasingly, stridently antisemitic in their politics. The German-Jewish alliance in Prague looks very much like a political marriage of convenience, yet it occurred and led to relatively good relations between Germans and Jews in the city. Moreover, even if it was based only on rational calculation, it is evidence that rational calculation is quite capable of overcoming the power of traditional prejudice.

A similar example is afforded by the case of late 19th-century Hungary. Hungary was one of the first countries in which antisemitism appeared as a modern political movement, as exemplified in the Tiszaeszlar Affair of 1882. Yet Hungary was also one of the first countries in which antisemitism was effectively suppressed in the pre-1914 era, and Hungary's capital, Budapest, was one of the most welcoming to Jews in Europe. This did not occur by accident. In the Austrian half of the Habsburg Monarchy and in Germany, the governments of Eduard Taaffe and Otto von Bismarck respectively tried to use the incipient antisemitic movement to apply pressure on the Austrian and German Jewish communities and their liberal allies, and hence allowed political antisemitism to develop and gain some respectability. In contrast, the Magyar gentry leadership that ruled Hungary quickly moved to counteract the antisemitic antics of the leading antisemitic politicians, Gyözö Istoczy and Ivan von Simonyi, so effectively that antisemitism was not a major concern for Hungarian Jews until shortly before 1914, and then in a much less threatening way than in Vienna and Austria.

The reasons for this relative failure of antisemitism in Hungary before 1914 are fairly clear: the Magyar political leadership calculated that the Magyar national cause would be much better served by coopting Hungarian Jewry, both as enthusiastic new members of the Magyar nation and as the group with the most capability for modernizing the Hungarian economy and hence giving the Magyar nation the economic power that was necessary to be taken seriously politically. Hence during the struggle for Hungarian autonomy from the 1840s into the 1860s, the Magyar leadership welcomed the largely voluntary Magyarization of Hungarian Jewry, especially in the western part of the kingdom and in Budapest, and it allowed and encouraged a Jewish bourgeoisie to develop in Pest that became the economic and financial powerhouse of the Hungarian nation state that was emerging *in nuce* in the Hungarian 'half' of Austria-Hungary from 1867 onwards. An attack on Hungarian Jewry thus was seen by the Magyar establishment, grouped in the Liberal Party, as an attack on one of the central pillars of the Magyar *national* cause. For reasons of national interest, therefore, the Tiszaeszlar case was dismissed and the antisemitic movement effectively silenced. Some authors have maintained that the Hungarian antisemitism of the early 1880s was the beginning of the road to the antisemitic measures of post-1918 Hungary, but this teleological viewpoint tends to ignore the fact that the era that followed was, as William McCagg pointed out, in many ways a Golden Age for Jews in Hungary, with remarkable social and economic advancement for many.

These examples show that, however deeply ingrained the prejudice against Jews might have been in the European, and especially Central European, mentality, this did not mean that this mindset could not change, or at least lead to other outcomes than full-blown antisemitism. The discourse originating in Christian anti-Judaism was only one of many competing ways Central Europeans had of interpreting the world in the late 19th century, and not necessarily the dominant one, even when it came to how to understand and behave towards Jews. The legacy of the Enlightenment (for all its ambivalences regarding Jews), the scientific revolution, and political change, together with the educative effect of empirical evidence, could, and in many instances did, dramatically alter attitudes to Jews in Europe by the late 19th century.

The prejudgement with which non-Jewish Europeans had inevitably made their 'first impression' about Jews was in most cases radically modified over time, over centuries indeed, and largely for the better. European Christians (and Christians elsewhere for that matter) might harbour suspicions and prejudices against Jews, as deniers of the Christian faith, or secular non-Jews might look askance at Jews as foreign and different, but these considerations had for the most part lost their cogency and been subordinated to others such as the need for tolerance, the uniting identity of a national political community, economic benefit, or simply the experience of personal interaction.

In some lands, however, and among certain groups, this anti-Jewish prejudice remained particularly strong, so strong that it could be turned by particular circumstances at a particular time into a political movement and ideology of its own: antisemitism.

The 'discourse' of prejudice was a necessary condition for antisemitism, but only part of the answer to its emergence. The other part to the answer lies in those particular circumstances in which an atavistic prejudice became the basis for a modern political movement. This involves looking at the historical context in which antisemitism arose in Central Europe, and it also involves looking at a particularly salient aspect of that context: the situation of European Jewry.

3. 'Jewish Pig', Wittenberg. The association of Jews with pigs became a staple of Central European anti-Jewish symbolism.

Chapter 3
The Chosen People

When antisemitism emerged as a political movement in the early 1880s, its ostensible adversary, European Jewry, had seen a radical transformation in its situation over the previous century or so. Knowledge of the nature and career of this transformation, and its varied geographic success, is crucial for understanding the career of antisemitism.

In the mid-18th century Jews in Europe had still lived largely apart from non-Jewish society in their own communities, corporate bodies in the corporately organized societies of the European *ancien régime*. The communal autonomy that this allowed was balanced by the consideration that Jews were regarded as inferior to their Christian counterparts in the social hierarchy, and often treated as such. Even at the end of the 18th century, Jews were still subject in much of Europe, especially in Central and Eastern Europe, to special taxes and prohibitions that were specifically designed to prostrate and humiliate, according to traditional Christian anti-Jewish doctrine.

The wave of modernization of the European economy, society, and political systems that spread from the western edge (Britain and Holland) from the mid-17th century, together with radical changes in thought encapsulated in the word 'Enlightenment', also radically altered attitudes to Jews. The switch from a corporate society to a modern 'Westphalian state' model, in which the sovereign ruled his subjects equally, according to rules of reason and without corporate, hierarchical structures, of necessity also required a profound change in the Jews' situation, and a need to integrate them into society in a much more direct way than previously, as individuals rather than as members of a quasi-separate community. The debate about how to effect this transformation of Jews to the benefit of the modernizing European states (and also the Jews themselves) came to be known as the 'Jewish Question'.

This 'Jewish Question' varied in intensity and character according to the nature and size of the Jewish communities in the various states, and to the way the integration of Jews into the larger society was initially handled. Integration of Jews into the original 'modern' societies of Western Europe went relatively smoothly. In Britain, where sovereign power (parliament) had long dominated over corporatist entities, the emphasis on individual rights under the rule of law, and a certain tolerance of difference, as well as a very small, mainly Sephardic, Jewish community, led to a relatively problem-free acceptance of Jews. This is not to say that there was complete silence on the issue, and there were at times vigorous debates on the need for Jews to reform and 'regenerate' themselves in order to fit in to British society, but the legal situation granting British-born Jews almost complete legal equality kept this discussion within bounds.

One ironic sign of the relative ease of Jewish integration in England was that there was not the same heroic tale to tell of Jewish emancipation as there was in France or especially Central Europe, and no definitive transformation of the Jews' legal status. Instead, change came, after the difficulties of 1753, incrementally, and in some aspects more slowly than on the Continent. Whereas Jews were given the right to attend and graduate from university in Austria in the late 18th century, it was only in 1870, with the University Test Act, that Jews were able to obtain degrees from

Oxford and Cambridge. Informal Jewish emancipation in England and broad social acceptance, had, however, been achieved decades before that, and was accompanied by many cases of religiously based philosemitism, even if some was based on evangelical hopes of a Second Coming. The 'Jewish Question' was rarely, if ever, of central import to British political culture, broad stereotypes of Disraeli in newspaper cartoons and a 'genteel' anti-Jewish snobbery in certain circles notwithstanding. In Italy, similarly, where there were ancient but relatively small Jewish communities, the 'Jewish Question' never became a central point of contention, and Jews participated fully in Italian society, culture, and politics with little comment or criticism.

France provides a somewhat different case, where the Bourbon *ancien régime* of the 18th century was not so amenable to the integration of Jews, although the Sephardic community centred in Bordeaux was much better viewed and treated than the Ashkenazi community centred in Alsace. A leading figure of the French Enlightenment, Voltaire, notoriously expressed a hostility to Jews and the Jewish religion. He was admittedly against all organized religion, but commentators such as Arthur Hertzberg have seen in Voltaire's hostility signs of a darker side of the Enlightenment that fed into later modern antisemitism. Nevertheless, Enlightened circles, led by Count Mirabeau, were also pressing for Jewish emancipation by the 1780s, and full Jewish emancipation was achieved as part of the Revolution in 1791. There was some back-sliding under Napoleon, whose 'Infamous Decrees' of 1808 attempted a forced integration of Alsatian Jews into French society and also attacked Jewish financial power by cancelling debts owed to Jews, but these decrees were allowed to lapse after the Bourbon restoration in 1815. Jews became full French citizens, and from 1831 the Jewish religion was put on an equal footing with the main Christian faiths. As in England, there might be considerable debate in the public sphere about whether Jews merited being regarded as Frenchmen, and many on the Catholic conservative Right denied this, but because the French state in the

4. 'A Propos de Judas Dreyfus', *La Libre Parole*, 10 November 1894.
Edouard Drumont catches Captain Alfred Dreyfus by his trousers.
Dreyfus's conviction of treason referred to here was not very
controversial; the Dreyfus Affair only gathered strength in 1898, when
Dreyfus's innocence became evident.

19th century held to the civic definition of membership of the French nation state, and Jews were accorded full rights as citizens, the 'Jewish Question' in France also remained relatively tame.

This might seem a strange assertion, given the prominence in the history of antisemitism (and Zionism) of the Dreyfus Affair, which concerned the false accusation of treason against the Jewish Captain Alfred Dreyfus, his conviction in 1894, and from 1898 the battle for his exoneration. The shock value of that Affair, however, came from precisely its unexpectedness, given the relatively uncontested nature of French Jewry's integration into general French society. The reactionary Catholic-monarchist, 'anti-Dreyfusard' sympathies revealed in large parts of the military establishment and many regions of France after the scandal really broke in 1898 were indeed a shocking challenge to the republican establishment, of which French Jews were mostly ardent supporters. The anti-Jewish riots that occurred during this period were evidence of the continuing strength of traditional (Catholic) anti-Jewish prejudice and the effect of the antisemitic campaigning of figures such as Edouard Drumont. Yet it was the Dreyfusards who won out, with Captain Alfred Dreyfus fully exonerated in 1906, and the Affair was always more a battle between traditional, Catholic-monarchist and revolutionary-republican versions of France than it was over France's 'Jewish Question'. In any case, once 'Progress' had won out, any question about French Jewry's status in France once again retreated to the far background, only to become a truly significant issue again after the Third Republic's collapse in 1940.

At the other end of Europe, in the Tsarist Russian Empire, the 'Jewish Question' was drastically different than in the rest of Europe, in as much as there was only ever partial emancipation of Jews under Tsarism. (Full emancipation came only with the February Revolution of 1917.) Unlike to the west, there was no extended period in 19th-century Russian history when an integration of the general Jewish population, on an individual basis as equal citizens, was undertaken by the state. There was no significant break between the traditional anti-Judaism of medieval Muscovy and the official hostility to Jews that continued to 1917. In that sense, Russian antisemitism was much more directly linked to traditional Christian anti-Judaism than was antisemitism to the west. Russian Muscovy, self-styled as the 'Third Rome', had prided itself on being free of Jews into the 18th century. It was only the annexation in the 18th century of vast tracts of the Polish-Lithuanian Commonwealth, where Jews had been allowed to settle for centuries, and which contained the vast bulk of Ashkenazi Jewry, that presented Tsarist authorities with a 'Jewish Problem'.

Traditional historiography has seen Russian policy towards its Jewish population in the 'Pale of Settlement' (former Poland-Lithuania) throughout the 19th century in terms of oppression, persecution, and discrimination. More recent studies, such as that of Heinz-Dietrich Löwe, have revised this somewhat, and pointed out the ways in which some 'enlightened absolutist', and even occasionally liberal, policies were attempted to integrate Jews into the Russian Empire's economy and society. The overall impression given by Tsarist Jewish policy, however, remains one based on ignorance, prejudice, and incompetence, ranging from general puzzlement about what to do with Jews to deep paranoia about what the Jews could do to Russian society. While the Tsarist authorities might not have been as malevolent as previously portrayed, the policies they ended up following were repressive, discriminatory, and often brutal.

Some attempts at coercive integration were made, as with the institution of compulsory military service, and some concessions made in various parts of the empire, such as in the post-1815 Kingdom of Poland and in the 'free city' of Odessa. Some privileged Jews, deemed 'useful' by the authorities, were allowed to reside outside the Pale, and even in St Petersburg and Moscow.

5. Victims from Kishinev (1903). The Kishinev pogrom, in which 49 Jews died, was regarded by international public opinion, and the international Jewish community, as a sign of Tsarist barbarism. Subsequent research has shown that Tsarist authorities were not directly implicated.

Some, such as the Poliakovs, became pioneers of Russian industrialization, and amongst this privileged group some selective integration did occur. Yet Jews generally remained a shunned and despised minority, by state and populace alike. Even the rule of Alexander II, the 'Tsar-Liberator', saw only modest reforms in Jewish policy, and his assassination in 1881 led to the wave of pogroms in the Pale that shocked Western opinion and accelerated the mass emigration of Russian Jews westward, most eventually to North America. After these pogroms, official policy towards Jews became *more* oppressive and restrictive, with, after a lull, more violence against Jews, such as the infamous Kishinev pogrom of 1903. The revolution of 1905 was followed by more anti-Jewish pogroms. The Russian right-wing movement of the Black Hundreds was very anti-Jewish, and the Tsarist government and its conservative supporters remained hostile to Jews until Tsarism's end in 1917.

Despite this hostile environment, the Russian Jewish community developed a modern political, social, and cultural life, and a considerable Jewish Russian-speaking intelligentsia also arose, especially among the privileged Jews allowed to reside outside the Pale and in exceptional communities such as Odessa. Yet even this acculturated Russian-speaking Jewish intelligentsia was set apart from Russian society proper, and generally modern Jewish life, especially within the Pale, remained within a Jewish context rather than a Russian one. It was in Russia that *cultural* Zionism developed, and among Russian Jews that the Zionist movement first arose, often as the result of the complete disillusionment, after 1881, of educated Jews who had still held out hope for Jewish emancipation in a modernizing Russia. Even the most successful brand of socialism within Russian Jewry, the Bund, was one which attempted to achieve internationalist integration of Russian Jewish workers through a Yiddish socialist sub-culture.

This lack of integration of Jews with the wider society was reflective of the form of Russian imperial, and national, identity. Within the Tsarist imperial thought structure, Jews remained both a despised religious minority and a separate ethnic group, along with all the other subject ethnicities of the empire. Sometimes classed as 'indigenous' alongside groups such as the Kalmuks; sometimes seen in terms of 'Semitic' religious groups, alongside Muslims and Tatars, they were not seen as an integral part of Russian society. The only way in which a Jew could 'become' Russian was the traditional, religiously sanctioned manner, by conversion to Russian Orthodox Christianity, and very few individuals took this path. Hence the classic 'Jewish Question', as understood in Western and Central Europe, of how and whether Jewish individuals could become fully integrated as members of the nation in which they lived, was never properly broached under Tsarism – because Jews, even fully 'Russified' Jews, were not seen as *nationally* Russian.

In other parts of Eastern Europe, there was a similar absence of accepting the emancipationist claim that Jews should be accepted primarily as individual citizens of the nation state. In Romania, the achievement of national independence after 1878 was, at the behest of the state's Western guarantors, premised on the granting of equal rights to minorities, meaning primarily Jews. Yet subsequent Romanian governments neatly sidestepped this condition by declaring that most of the Jews in Romania were 'foreign' and hence not Romanian citizens. In the Polish kingdom (ruled by Russia), Jews officially had 'equal rights', but the dominant Polish political party there, the National Democrats (Endeks), led by Roman Dmowski, similarly saw Jews as a foreign, economically parasitical presence among the Polish nation, and instigated an economic boycott against them.

In Austrian Galicia, Polish nationalism took a similar approach to Jews in the 1890s, with pogroms and attempts at economic boycott, led by Father Stanislaw Stojalowski. Although Galician Jews were officially, as citizens of the Austrian half of the Habsburg Dual Monarchy, fully emancipated, equal citizens, the backward social and economic structures in most of Galicia had perpetuated the more corporatist model of separate Jewish communities among a largely peasant Polish and Ukrainian populace. Jews had preserved their own social and religious organization and along with this went a distinct ethnic and cultural identity; they were therefore far from integrated, and were quite easily seen by the rest of society as a foreign entity in the 'organic' nation. The 'Jewish Question' in Galicia therefore showed more similarities with the Russian model in social and cultural terms than with the Western or Central European version, even though Galicia was part of politically 'Western' Austria-Hungary. Polish 'antisemitism' similarly had far more direct links with traditional Catholic anti-Judaism than the 'modern' antisemitism to the West.

For those who view antisemitism as the direct product of traditional anti-Jewish hostility, stemming from the Catholic Christian and, for Russia, Orthodox Christian pre-modern traditions, Eastern Europe would seem to prove the direct connection. Yet it was not in Russia that *modern* antisemitism was founded. Russians did make some decisive contributions to the success of antisemitism, such as the final version of the *Protocols of the Elders of Zion*, but even this document, in its conspiratorial view of the world, was informed with a pre-modern mentality. The anti-Jewish mindset of the Tsarist authorities was very well known throughout the 19th century and was regarded, smugly perhaps, as merely a sign of backwardness. Even when a form of ideological Russian antisemitism did develop, it was, as Löwe has described it, a 'reactionary Utopia', the 'pre-modern' ideology of a backward-looking 'old elite'. It is ironic, given the vehemence of Tsarist hostility to Jews before the regime's fall in 1917, that Russian antisemitism's ties with Russian traditionalist agrarian values, traditional Jew-hatred, and the Tsarist establishment, might also explain why it did not contribute directly to the Holocaust.

The region where modern antisemitism arose, and where the plans for the Holocaust were hatched, was also the region where the 'Jewish Question' was both asked and yet also waited interminably for an answer: Central Europe. The 'Jewish Question' remained potent in German-dominated Central Europe due to the way in which the initial argument for the integration of Jews, and their emancipation from pre-modern discriminations, was framed. Whereas in Western Europe, emancipation was based mainly on the principle of individual human rights, which were deemed to be inherently due to Jews as citizens and human beings, in Central Europe Jewish emancipation came early on to be seen in terms of what David Sorkin has described as a grand *quid pro quo*: Jews would be given their rights once they had proven they could earn them. That is to say, Jews would have to deserve their claim to equal treatment by giving up their 'Jewish' ways which Christian

Germans found so repellent. Indeed, the implicit bargain of Jewish emancipation, from the viewpoint of the non-Jewish, still Christian state at the turn of the 19th century, was that full Jewish integration into society would involve total assimilation. Jews would, in leaving behind their negative 'Jewish' particularities, leave behind all markers of Jewish difference, and become indistinguishable from their Christian German counterparts. C. W. Dohm was actually an advocate for emancipating the Jews as their right, but in describing the beneficial consequences of that action he summed up the implicit promise that was to dominate the rationale for Jewish emancipation when he declared: 'Let them cease to be Jews!'

From the state's viewpoint, the integration of Jews into society and the economy was justified because of the needs of the state: for administrative uniformity and to encourage economic growth. Individual Jews were to be freed from some of the most oppressive restrictions against them, but in return were expected to contribute directly to the state, in the form of military service, surrender their right to communal autonomy, and give up their separate cultural identity. Hence the most famous advance in Jewish policy in Central Europe before 1789, the set of Toleration Edicts of Emperor Joseph II for the Habsburg lands from 1781 onwards, was as much an attack on Jewish communal rights as it was an alleviation of restrictions on Jews. It was, moreover, explicitly intended 'to make the totality of Jewry harmless, but the individual useful'. In this regard, it is important to note that many very inhumane restrictions on Jews, such as the Familiant Laws that limited marriage to the eldest sons of Jewish families in Bohemia, were not abolished by Joseph II and remained on the books until the mid-19th century. Meanwhile, the tutelary state was to remake the Jews in its own image. The new German-language schools for Jews that Joseph II's policies instituted in Bohemia were intended to make the Jews more useful, because more easy to integrate into non-Jewish society and the economy, but they were also intended to make Jews less

'Jewish' and more like model, ethnically neutral, 'Austrian' citizens – theoretically like everyone else.

Policy in Prussia and most other German states was similar. The French revolutionary conquest and reorganization of Germany in the 1800s provided a temporary anticipation of a full, French-style emancipation of Jews on the basis of individual rights, but the expulsion of the French invader meant in the case of most German states a rescinding of newly gained Jewish rights (and an identification of the Jewish beneficiaries of French policy with the French national enemy). Prussia conferred citizenship on Prussian Jews in 1812, but this did not mean full civic equality, and the promise of full emancipation was repeatedly deferred after 1815, as the authorities remained unconvinced that Jews *deserved* what appeared to them the privilege of equality. Civic equality was eventually granted in Prussia in April 1848 (after the 1848 revolution) and other German states followed suit, some faster than others. It was only with the formation of the North German Confederation in 1869 and the German Empire in 1871 that German Jews gained full legal emancipation. Meanwhile, in the Habsburg Monarchy, Jews similarly gained their emancipation in the wake of the 1848 revolution, only to have it snatched away again when Emperor Francis Joseph decided not to confirm it as part of the absolutist Sylvester Patent of 1851–2. Jews had to wait until 1860 to gain such rights as the right to real property ownership, and full legal emancipation of Jews in Cisleithania (the Austrian half of the Dual Austro-Hungarian Monarchy) had to wait until 1867.

Moses Mendelssohn, the leader in Berlin of the *Haskalah*, the Jewish Enlightenment, had initially argued for Jewish equality as a matter of right and, while advocating acculturation and integration into German culture and society, was wary of more comprehensive assimilation. His successors in the leadership of the emancipation movement in German Central Europe, however, appeared, on one level, to accept the states' *quid pro quo* of emancipation in return for total assimilation and the disappearance of Jewish difference. David Friedländer explicitly argued that emancipation would lead to the regeneration of German Jewry, and their speedy integration into German society. Disappointed at the failure of Prussia to grant immediate emancipation, Friedländer even proposed in 1799 that the family heads of Berlin Jewry give up their separate Jewish faith and convert to Protestantism, albeit with the proviso that the Protestants not insist on the irrational belief in the Trinity.

This radical measure was rejected out of hand, by Jew and Christian alike, and would be a mere historical oddity if it did not reveal the gulf that remained between the Jewish and Christian perspectives of what emancipation and integration, even assimilation, entailed. Both Mendelssohn and Friedländer continued to insist on Jews having a prior right to emancipation, and saw integration as a two-way process, in which Jews and Christians could share values common to both religions. Later ideologues of emancipation, ever more desperate to achieve equal civil rights for Jews, did come to accept the *quid pro quo* set by the German states. Campaigners such as Gabriel Riesser, intent on disarming non-Jews' suspicions that Jews still constituted a 'state within a state', proclaimed any separate Jewish national identity long deceased, and argued for rights for Jews as patriotic Germans who differed from their co-nationals only in the private matter of religious confession. The leadership of German Central Europe's Jewish communities established many organizations to achieve the cultural and moral regeneration of Jews through the tenets of German humanist *Bildung* (roughly translatable as 'educative development of the self'). Societies were established to persuade Jews to follow 'respectable' trades, and even engage in agriculture. The clear assumption was that by Jews fulfilling their side of the bargain by acculturating and assimilating into German society, they would eventually be rewarded by being officially accepted as full citizens, because they had in reality become fully German, indistinguishable in manner, culture, and appearance from other

Germans. Yet Jews remained different, they remained an identifiable group within German society, and this was partly because of the very effort, sustained for almost a century, to overcome their difference.

In many respects, the drive for emancipation and the ideology of self-improvement that informed it were remarkably successful. Jews in Germany in 1780, apart from the group of wealthy financiers and war contractors, went from being a mainly economically deprived and culturally isolated set of outcasts, to by 1880, apart from the group of very wealthy financiers and industrialists, consisting mainly of a respectable and prosperous bourgeoisie, with a far higher degree of education than the general German populace. In Austria-Hungary it is arguable that the social transformation was not quite so radical, given the Galician circumstances, and there appears to have been many poor, even destitute Jews in Vienna around 1900, for instance. At the same time, a large sector of Austrian Jewry had also made remarkable social and economic strides, which the family history of Sigmund Freud exemplifies. German Central European Jewry espoused the apparent social values of the rest of the German propertied and educated middle classes (*Bildungs- und Besitzbürgertum*) and were ardent patriots of their respective states (the German Empire and Austria-Hungary), albeit under a liberal, constitutional interpretation. In other words, the social and economic identity of German Central European Jewry changed radically, and in many ways there was a large degree of successful integration. Yet Jews did not cease to be different as the advocates of emancipation had predicted.

If Jews went from being beggars and pedlars to being merchants and businessmen, itinerant Talmudic scholars to journalists and writers, this represented an increase in respectability and integration, perhaps, but it still left the Jewish occupational structure, and hence its socio-economic 'identity', looking quite different from that of society at large. Partly this was because of continuing *de facto* limits on Jewish career options, most notoriously an informal bar on the higher posts within the various state bureaucracies without the 'necessary' baptismal certificate. Efforts to create a large cadre of Jewish artisans also petered out due to resistance from the Christian artisans and their guild organizations, and efforts to attract Jews to agrarian pursuits were also largely fruitless. Jewish traditions and attitudes, however, also played a large role, especially the traditional stress among Jewish families on the importance of education. The new modern Jewish dispensation simply transferred this high valuation from the religious to the secular sphere. The result was that there was a large 'over-representation' of Jews in finance, commerce, many export-oriented and innovation-based branches of industry, the professions, modern literature, and modern culture generally.

Moreover, Jews continued to maintain their own religious identity, and the newly prosperous, integrated, and acculturated modern Jewish communities, in Berlin, Vienna, Budapest, Breslau, and elsewhere reconfirmed this religious identity in dramatic, concrete terms, in majestic 'temples', often in 'Orientalist' Moorish style that looked back to the idyllic age of medieval Sephardic Jewry, that dominated their immediate urban landscape. Religious identity was thus not merely a 'private' matter, and even if Jews were attending services reformed along Protestant lines, as good German bourgeois, they were attending their own separate and different 'church'. This was a quite dramatically different outcome from that envisaged by many non-Jewish advocates of emancipation, at its inception and also much later in the century, who had assumed that Jewish acculturation and integration would inevitably lead also to a giving up of the 'atavistic' Jewish religion in favour of modern Christianity, in Germany especially the 'cultural Protestantism' of the academic elite. There were many conversions away from Judaism, and especially in the elite economic and cultural circles, with figures such as Felix Mendelssohn-Bartholdy and Heinrich Heine leading a stellar cast of such Jewish converts in German and Austrian culture, yet the vast bulk of Central European Jewry did not convert and remained Jews in whatever form, even if it was, as in Sigmund Freud's case, as a 'godless Jew'.

To some extent a distinct politico-cultural Jewish identity also persisted. The very struggle for emancipation, over almost a century, had created a large panoply of organizations to 'reform' Jewish society, and these social bodies and networks continued to exist after emancipation was achieved, producing a Jewish form of civil society and hence a Jewish social identity. The long fight for emancipation had also produced its own ideology, centred on the concept of *Bildung*, both as a form of intellectual and moral development. It also, logically, held a faith in the universal benefit of emancipation, of liberation of the individual human being from the constraints of irrational past oppression and superstition. Jews in Germany and Austria therefore tended very much to vote for the upholders of 'emancipation', whether Jewish or otherwise, which usually meant the progressive Left, in other words usually the Liberals or their equivalent, and later the Social Democrats. Culturally and politically, this emancipatory tradition provided Jews with an overall profile that differed quite markedly from the non-Jewish part of German and Austrian society, and produced an identifiable Jewish 'sub-culture' in German Central European society. Jews did not 'disappear' into German and Austrian society as had been predicted.

In retrospect, this Jewish 'difference', socially, culturally, and economically, might have been expected, and somewhat similar social and economic patterns were evident in Western European countries as well. Yet in Central Europe the emancipation of Jews had come to be predicated on the promise of total absorption of those Jews into the larger society. When the persistence of Jewish difference showed that the promise had not been met, this allowed the liberal project of Jewish emancipation to be labelled a failure by conservatives. The perpetuation of this mindset of having total assimilation of Jews, their effective disappearance, as the ultimate goal of their emancipation, also led to a continued insistence by emancipation's defenders, whether liberals, progressives, or socialists, Jews or non-Jews, on the idea that Jews were no different from other Germans and Austrians. Jews were not defended for what they were, but for what they were not. This defence on the basis of denial drastically hobbled attempts to combat antisemitism, for conservatives, and antisemites could point very persuasively to evidence that Jews were in fact different in many ways, despite what Jews and their emancipationist allies might claim. The irony was that the very ideology of emancipation, with its claims to a universal humanity, was a major reason why emancipatory Jews, seeing themselves in those universalist terms, could not see, or admit, their own difference.

The framing of emancipation as a *quid pro quo* with total assimilation, and the persistence of the 'Jewish Question' for almost a century, clearly paved the way for the effectiveness of antisemitic counter-arguments against Jewish emancipation. In effect, the framing of the 'Question' meant that even one of the most successful and productive integrations of an ethno-religious minority in all of history could nevertheless be labelled a dismal failure, and believed to have been as such. In itself, however, the persistence of Jewish difference, and the recognition of this, even in the form of ethnic hostility, does not necessarily explain the flourishing of antisemitism as a political force. It helps to explain, but it is not sufficient. It also does not explain why Jewish difference was still seen as quite so deleterious and even threatening by so many Germans and Central Europeans. Perhaps if we look at what the protagonists of emancipation were up against in terms of Central European society and culture, we will get a stage further.

Chapter 4
The culture of irrationalism

Antisemitism has been defined by many scholars as irrational hostility to Jews. This definition's adequacy is debatable, but it is quite clear that antisemitism has usually been seen as linked to the irrational, non-rational, or anti-rational in some way. The emergence of political and ideological antisemitism in German Central Europe in the late 19th century has often been linked by historians to the culture of 'irrationalism'. This cultural approach was not in itself irrational, rather it was a reaction against the rationalist claim that all of human experience and endeavour could be reduced to rational, calculable objects and relations, and should be. Irrationalists, in contrast, asserted that there was a place for 'irrational' emotions and imagination in art and life, that these indeed were part of a realm superior to mere reason. Starting with Romanticism, the 'irrationalist' revolt against rationalist modernity was influential throughout European culture and thought from the late 18th century onwards. In Britain, William Blake, in his hatred of unfeeling 'Urizen', the god of abstract reason, was clearly part of this cultural movement, and even an august liberal such as John Stuart Mill rebelled against the equating of poetry and pushpin, as rationalist utilitarianism prescribed; but irrationalism was particularly influential in German culture.

There was a quite strong link between German cultural 'irrationalism' and antisemitism. Many of the representative figures of cultural 'irrationalism' in Germany, such as Arthur Schopenhauer and Richard Wagner, disliked Jews, and many antisemites were followers of 'irrationalist' culture. In retrospect, it is quite easy to see how this linkage developed, and how it became so effective: it originated from the view that Jews were connected to detested rationalist modernity, and there was plenty of evidence for this idea. As we have seen, the movement for Jewish emancipation, in itself a response to the rationalization and modernization of European states, meant that Jews in German Central Europe did indeed become closely allied to the goals of rationalist modernity; but not in the way in which antisemites claimed.

Jews had accepted the *quid pro quo* of integration into the rational modern state in return for emancipation, and had therefore striven to become rationally 'useful' members of society. Their support for rationalist modernity was thus based on the acceptance of their side of the bargain with the non-Jewish state and, they thought, society. Once the new, modernized Jewish identity had been formed, however, German society had moved on from the Enlightened model of the rational state, and many Germans had indeed revolted against this 'soulless' version of social organization. Antisemites and 'irrationalists' thus came to assert, with some foundation, that there was still a Jewish 'difference', and they characterized this by emphasizing the Jews' continued allegiance to rationalist modernity. Some saw the irony of this as a result of the Jews' very attempt to integrate into German society; however, many antisemites attributed rationalist modernity itself to the Jews, seeing it as the product of an essentially rational and abstract 'Jewishness' (*Judentum*) that was, in its analytically critical approach, undermining and destroying traditional, 'organic' native (i.e. national) society. From being prompted, even coerced, into becoming part of rational, modern society and state in Central Europe, Jews came, partly as a result of their very success in this effort at modernizing, to be regarded as in the 'vanguard' of rationalist modernity; and then, when this ceased to be a popular cause, as the *instigators* of that rationalist modernity.

Romanticism in Germany was a revolt against what was seen as the immorality, superficiality, and lack of profundity of the (French) Enlightenment, and a protest against the soulless and Nature-destroying character of (English) industrialization. From early on it was also closely linked with German nationalism, and this relationship became even closer in the wake of the French Revolution and the French invasion and conquest of the German states in the early 19th century. The traumatic collapse of the German states system of the Holy Roman Empire and radical French-induced reform did not last long. Napoleon's defeat meant that by 1815 a quasi-traditional states system, the German Confederation, had substituted for the pre-revolutionary German polity. Yet the intervening years had a substantial effect on the character of Romantic German nationalism, making it both much more radically anti-French, and, because Jews had been one of the most prominent beneficiaries of French liberalization, more anti-Jewish. Moses Mendelssohn and the Berlin Jewish elite had initially succeeded at being accepted by the Prussian cultural elite, on rationalist lines, as civilized human beings and German civic 'patriots'. This was undermined by the Romantic notion that Jews, not being part of the German national body, could never become fully German, and would always, therefore, be a foreign entity within the nation. A notorious instance of this kind of thought was that of the idealist philosopher, and German nationalist, Johann Gottlieb Fichte, and his hostility to Jews as an alien entity was shared by the father of multiculturalism, Johann Gottlieb von Herder, although in a milder form.

The main German advance in thought, the idealism founded by Immanuel Kant, also developed in ways deleterious to full acceptance of Jews. Kant himself had displayed his own prejudiced understanding of the Jewish religion by classifying it as a heteronomous religion, which consisted of the individual only obeying laws imposed on him, not those he recognized by the light of his own reason through the categorical imperative. Yet many Jewish thinkers dismissed this as a travesty of Jewish religion and ethics, based on Kant's ignorance of Judaism. They concentrated instead on the great similarities between Kantian and Jewish thought, and the possibilities that the idea of an ethics of the autonomous will opened up for a rational organization of society, in which Jewish individuals would be equal with all other autonomous individual citizens. Kant became a guiding light for many of the greatest German Jewish thinkers, including Hermann Cohen.

Yet philosophical idealism after Kant left its Enlightened, rationalist moorings and developed in parallel to Romanticism's emphasis on the irrational and the emotional, on the concept of the will, first in figures such as Fichte and later in the work of Arthur Schopenhauer. Schopenhauer's pessimism set the world of cause and effect, and of the purposive pursuit of self-interest, the world of mere empirical 'representation', against the noumenal world of pure will. He identified the latter with the purely spiritual, the real natural world beyond the perverse perspective of rationalism. The noumenal world could only be realized by self-abnegation in the sordid world of empirical reality and an ethics of compassion. As with Kant, Schopenhauer saw Judaism as an example of the heteronomous obedience to external entities, the reverse of his ideal of compassion, and as indeed the prime cause for the artificial division between Man and Nature that he saw as the fundamental, tragic dichotomy in the Western view of reality. Apart from holding a host of traditional prejudices against Jews, Schopenhauer thus held to a strong theoretical anti-Judaism, as he understood Jewish religion. In many ways, as with Kant and Fichte, Schopenhauer's hostility to Jews derived from the Christian doctrine of Jewish blindness in the face of

Christ's divinity and the traditional theological concept of Judaism being a religion of mere obedience to law, lacking Christian 'love', but it was also a protest against both the results of economic and social modernization *and* a rejection of traditional Christianity.

The ultimate figure of mid-to-late 19th-century German culture, of a nationalist, irrationalist, neo-Romantic kind, but also simultaneously 'modern' and antisemitic, was Richard Wagner. It is clear that Wagner was antisemitic in his thought. As early as 1850 he anonymously published a long pamphlet, *Das Judentum in der Musik*, in which he attacked the artificiality of the music of successful Jewish composers of the time such as Giacomo Meyerbeer. Wagner claimed that Jews, born outside the German nation, could never learn to express themselves authentically, either linguistically or musically, because art was not something that could be learned mechanically, but came from the national spirit. He also bewailed the commercialization of the modern German music world, and attributed this to both the sickness of modern German culture and society, and the materialistic nature of Jews, who were simply interested in selling their 'artistic wares' rather than expressing true art.

Wagner was, in other words, expressing Schopenhauerian, anti-Jewish thought in a social theory about music. Wagner's antisemitism, expressed anonymously, was not immediately known to the public, and it was only when he published his antisemitic pamphlet in 1869 under his own name that his views became known as his to that public. Wagner published several subsequent articles with an antisemitic component. Today, as in his own day, many admirers of Wagner's music insist that his great musical works, such as the *Ring* cycle and *Parsifal*, are not in themselves antisemitic. Yet figures such as Alberich, the dwarf who steals the Ring of the Nibelungs, appear to fit all too easily in the context of Wagner's Romantic, Schopenhauerian mindset as 'Jewish' stereotypes. In this world view, greed and selfishness, the drive of the sub-human to dominion over the world, and a lack of

6. Arthur Rackham, 'The Rhinemaidens Teasing Alberich' (1911). The character Alberich in Richard Wagner's *The Ring of the Nibelungen* has been seen as a cipher of the composer's antisemitic ideology.

understanding of higher spirituality, are all attributed to the distorted world of Western 'representation' that has its origins in the Old Testament and finds its modern embodiment in the profit-obsessed world of 'Jewish' modern capitalism. Wagner did not detest Jewish commercialization only: after a trip along the Thames between London and Greenwich, Wagner remarked that what he had seen was 'Alberich's dream'. The English obsession with material gain, however, was for Wagner yet another instance of the 'Judaization' (*Verjudung*) of the world.

The association of Jews with money was also of centuries-old vintage, and fitted neatly into German irrationalism's contempt for the self-interested, materialistic values of the modern capitalist economy. Jews were thus seen as being a demoralizing, amoral group, only interested in their own advancement, regardless of the problems this might cause for the upstanding native German population, whose nation was 'too young' to resist this perverting, despiritualizing influence of alien Jews, 'multitudes of assiduous pant-selling youths' from Poland, and literary 'Semitic hustlers', as Heinrich Treitschke put it in 1879. A few years earlier, in 1875, another august professor, Theodor Billroth, had made a very similar argument in Vienna about the bad influence of too many alien and poor Jews flooding in from Galicia with the aim to earn money from medicine, rather than adopting medicine as a vocation. In both instances, a prime audience was the very nationalistic student body, who put the nation above the sordid reality of industrializing society and political deal-making, as something spiritually pure and beyond mere rationalist, empirical modernity, and hence as something from which Jews, as the embodiment of such things in the irrationalist canon, should be excluded.

Even irrationalist thinkers who opposed antisemitism, and nationalism, such as Friedrich Nietzsche, also contributed, almost against their will, to the antisemitic thrust of German irrationalist culture. While his real target of opprobrium was organized

Christianity for perpetuating a 'slave morality' against the 'natural' value system of ancient Greece that valued strength, youth, beauty, and 'power', Nietzsche inevitably followed his irrationalist predecessors in seeing the origins of this 'slave morality' in the 'heteronomous' religion of Old Testament Judaism. Nietzsche often praised modern emancipated Jews as a beneficial influence on European civilization. Yet his fulminations against the originally Jewish 'slave morality' that was resisting his proposed transvaluation of values could easily be abused to target modern Jews as the obstacle to human liberation, a liberation that could also be seen as one from the oppressive morality of the heteronomous, rationalist modernity of capitalism's deferred gratification and its reining in of humanity's more 'animal' feelings and instincts. Whether as amoral, immoral, or too moral, Jews were despised by German irrationalist culture, because their 'rationalism' made them blind to the truly spiritual nature of the German essence, or so it seemed.

The problem for Jews with this broad irrationalist critique, supported by some of the central figures of 19th-century German national culture, was twofold. First, it struck at the heart of the rationale of their emancipation. This had depended on the idea of Man as a rational, moral, and educable agent, who would act in his own self-interest and by the light of reason, hence recognizing the inherent humanity of other peoples, such as Jews. At least this viewpoint allowed those others (Jews) to improve themselves to the level of rationality and culture sufficient to merit being full members of society. Religious and ethnic differences would ultimately be ironed out by rational debate and empirical evidence, as the Ring Fable in Gotthold Ephraim Lessing's *Nathan the Wise* suggested. In the German case, this was assumed to mean that Jews would acculturate as Germans and as such be indistinguishable from other rational, German-speaking citizens of the rational state. The irrationalist critique completely undermined this rationale, because it denied that Man was primarily a rational being, and it made full membership of society dependent on things beyond mere rational, empirical actions, such as adherence to the laws and education in the mores, language, and culture. Rather, membership now required belonging in a national community that at times took on mystical overtones, and often was defined in terms of shared 'blood and soil'. Following Romanticism, German nationality was something inherited rather than learned, given not acquirable, a matter of feeling rather than rationality. Although the terminology came later, irrationalist culture from the early 19th century defined German nationality in terms of a 'community' (*Gemeinschaft*) rather than a 'society' (*Gesellschaft*); Jews, having been the traditional outsiders of German society for centuries, found it nigh impossible to enter the former, whereas as rational individuals their way into the latter had seemed wide open.

Second, the irrationalist critique was difficult for Jews to refute because it mirrored, albeit distortedly, enough of social and cultural reality to be at least partly credible, especially in German Central Europe. Emancipated Jews not only were identified with Enlightenment, liberalism, and the modern, rational capitalist economy by non-Jewish society; they themselves identified with these ideals. The very ideology of emancipation made such an identification virtually inevitable, given its goal of making Jews suitable for integration into modern society. Adolf Jellinek, Vienna's leading rabbi in the Liberal Era and a prominent spokesman for emancipation, stressed in 1861 the compatibility of Jews and the Jewish religion with the 'new time' of modernity. He compared the Jewish character to that of the English, with a firm foundation of tradition allowing greater opportunity to change and evolve. Jellinek particularly emphasized the Jews' combination of an analytic mind and a very purposive individualism, and asserted that modern society ought to be just to Jews because it was taking on Jewish 'qualities'. This sort of ethnic triumphalism was perhaps understandable as an exercise in emancipationist apologetics, but it all too easily fed into anti-Jewish paranoia. One of Wagner's most vitriolic anti-Jewish tracts, 'Modern', appears to have been a direct response to an article by a Jewish apologist making the same kind of positive connection between Jews and modernity. An ironic echo of this identification can be seen in Theodor Herzl's Zionist diary, when he says that his aim is to make a 'modern people', the Jews, into the most modern in the world.

There was, moreover, circumstantial economic and cultural evidence that by the second half of the 19th century bolstered this claim to a special relationship of Jews to modernity. Jews were indeed very prominent in the German Central European modern economy and modern culture. The claim by many antisemites that Jews had invented this economy and culture was false. Although court Jews had played their part as financiers and war contractors in Central Europe's early modern economy, the origins of the modern, capitalist economy lay primarily elsewhere. That Jews were so well placed and so ready to take advantage of the opportunities afforded by the new economy was ironically at least partly due to their marginalization by anti-Jewish discrimination in the traditional, agrarian economy. The fact remains that for such a small minority (less than 1% of Germany's population, and less than 5% of Austria-Hungary's), Jews had a remarkably large role in many leading fields of the 19th century's modern industrial economy. These included finance (a traditional area, admittedly), development of the railway system, textile manufacturing, and later electrical machinery, transatlantic shipping, and large-scale clothing retail, especially that symbol of modern commercialism, the department store. Similarly, a pantheon of cultural and intellectual figures – from Felix Mendelssohn-Bartholdy, Heinrich Heine, and Ludwig Börne at one end, to Arnold Schoenberg, Franz Kafka, Sigmund Freud, and Albert Einstein at the other – provided an immense Jewish participation in modern culture in German Central Europe. A cultural irrationalist or conservative nationalist in late 19th-century Central Europe, opposed to and threatened by rationalist modernity, would easily have associated Jews with what he feared and detested, because

7. 'Inexplicable what one experiences', *Kikeriki*, 9 September 1883. Kikeriki cartoon: 'Thus and not other wise did their fathers appear! And today the sons of such Polish Jews want to teach us Viennese about Germanness!'

most Jews in German Central Europe, the products of the movement for emancipation, were in reality upholders of the ideals of the Enlightenment, liberalism, and progress, in other words of rationalist modernity.

When, therefore, the protest against rationalist modernity gained momentum in the later 19th century, Jews were an obvious candidate for scapegoating. The protest had been fuelled both by disappointment with the negative consequences of 'Manchester-style' unrestrained economic growth in environmental degradation and threatening, unhealthy urban centres, and by the increase in prestige of nationalism as the organicist, 'irrationalist' answer to the alienation and anomie of the emerging industrial society. Jews had not been the cause of rationalist modernity, or of modernity's failings, but they had come to be among modernity's closest allies and they suffered when it came under attack.

In France, antisemites such as Edouard Drumont attacked Jews initially for their role in finance and, supposedly, the financial corruption of the Third Republic. Drumont's first major success came in the Panama Scandal of 1892–3, when outrage at a national humiliation was diverted, by Drumont's agitation, onto two Jewish speculators, and hence onto all of 'Jewish France'. French antisemitism reached its height during the Dreyfus Affair. This was an argument less about French Jews than about the French Revolution, and whether the republican, anti-clerical Left, or the conservative, Catholic Right ruled France. Yet Dreyfus's Jewishness, and the fact that he was on the General Staff at all, was deeply symbolic of the Revolution's meritocratic and egalitarian ideals. It was at the same time what had made Dreyfus appear an easy victim to frame, and it was also the apparent weak point through which French conservative and reactionary forces had thought to undermine the progressive Left. Dreyfus and his cause came not only to represent French Jewry but also rational, modern France. In this French case the Dreyfusards, French Jewry, and rationalist, progressive modernity won out over traditional conservatism and Catholicism, and irrationalists such as Drumont or Maurice Barrès.

In the Russian Empire, in contrast, rationalist modernity never stood much of a chance in the social and political, or even cultural, sphere. Economic modernization in the form of industrialization did become a top Tsarist priority in order to maintain Russia's position in the international system, and this priority was one of the main reasons for the emancipation of the serfs in 1861. Yet it always ran up against the deeply conservative (and contradictory) desire of the Tsarist regime and much of Russian public opinion to protect Russia's largely agrarian society and traditional cultural values from the consequences of capitalism. And early on Russian conservatives identified 'capitalism' with 'the Jews'. That this identification percolated down to the popular level is one explanation for why the social unrest that occurred in the wake of the emancipation eventually came to express itself after Alexander II's assassination in 1881 in pogroms against Jews. Similarly in 1905, when revolution threatened to undermine Tsarist power, nationalists and reactionaries rallied around authority and one result was a new round of pogroms against Jews. The fact that increasing numbers of Jews, especially in the Bund, were supporters of radical social and economic change, and that Jews were heavily represented in the ranks of the Marxist socialist leadership (Bolshevik and Menshevik) only served to heighten the sense that Jews were the enemies of Tsarist authority and traditional Russian values, as both capitalists *and* socialists.

In many areas of the late 19th-century Habsburg Monarchy as well, nationalist remedies for the consequences of economic modernization and national competition, whether in Polish Western Galicia or amongst Czechs and Germans in Bohemia, could often result in Jews being attacked instead. In Vienna, Jews were attacked for the distress caused by the modern economy on traditional trades and handicrafts, and in Germany political antisemitism scored some of its greatest victories in depressed rural areas, where Jewish cattle traders became the focus of blame for larger economic trends for which those traders were not directly responsible. On the more general level, Jews were not responsible for the problems created by the modern economy, and many Jews also suffered from those problems. Yet, overall Jews were obvious beneficiaries of economic change, and as such they were seen, almost inevitably, as part of the mysterious, new capitalist system that was threatening the livelihood of so many non-Jews.

Jews, as allies of modernity, thus became the targets of many of those in Central and Eastern Europe who suffered from the dislocations of economic modernization and the loss of moral and spiritual certitude that came with what Max Weber called the 'dis-enchantment of the world', modernity's undermining and dismantling of the traditional authority embodied in the hierarchical social order, the Church and the Monarchy.

Antisemites who came to their hostility to Jews from the 'irrationalist', conservative, and traditionalist viewpoint often regarded both capitalism and socialism as 'Jewish'. This tendency has often been cited as proof of the complete irrationality of irrationalist antisemitism. Yet blaming both sides of the central econo-political conflict of modern history on Jews was not as irrational as it might appear. The relationship between the socialist opponents of the modern, capitalist economy and Jews was a complex and ambivalent one. There was indeed a tradition of anti-Jewish hostility on the radical French Left in the early 19th century, among such figures as Charles Fourier, Pierre-Joseph Proudhon, and especially Fourier's disciple Alphonse Toussenel, who attacked the Jews as the spirit behind the 'financial feudality' exploiting the French people. In Germany as well, radical left-wing thought was often bracketed with anti-Jewish hostility, even when it was not ostensibly anti-Jewish. Bruno Bauer in 1843 used the debate over the 'Jewish Question' to launch a radically anti-clerical critique of all religion. In the course of this attack on religion, Bauer made the claim that Jews would only be successfully emancipated when they, along with all Christians, gave up their religion, because all religion was a 'chimera' standing in the way of human progress, fraternity, and enlightenment.

This radical version of the argument of emancipation as equal to the disappearance of all Jewish difference was taken up in an even more notorious essay, by the young Karl Marx in *On the Jewish Problem* of 1844, in which Marx faulted Bauer not for wanting Jews to give up their separate identity, but rather for seeing the problem as one of religion rather than of the material money-economy, which Marx, at this point, equates with 'Judaism' (*Judentum*). For Marx, true emancipation, for Jews and all others, will come when the tyranny of the money-economy, Judaism, is cast off by Mankind.

The anti-Jewish character of even the young Marx's early socialism would seem to make the later antisemitic attack on socialism as 'Jewish' truly irrational. Yet Marxist socialism, as it developed in the second half of the 19th century, became a quite different ideology. Even in 1848, Marx's theory was of communism as the inevitable, *modern* outcome of the dialectics within capitalism. Sitting in exile in London, Marx melded his Hegelianism with very empiricist Ricardian economic theory, conducting an internal critique of British capitalism, and thus produced a mature theory that depended on rational self-interest as its engine. Marx thus combined an ethical critique of modern capitalism with the outlook of rationalist modernity, seeing his communism not as a reaction but a development of the modern economy. Just like advocates of 'Manchesterist' capitalism, Marxism had no interest in preserving useless traditional vestiges of authority – in that sense, the irrationalist antisemites were quite correct in seeing both capitalism and Marxist socialism as threatening 'traditional' forms of society, because they were two sides of the same coin. As such, they were both on a different, modern plane from the pre-modern forms of artisanry and agriculture which still typified large swathes of the European economy in the late 19th century.

It was therefore not irrational to see capitalism and socialism as linked in the way that irrationalist, conservative antisemites imagined. Nor was it entirely illusory to see both as 'Jewish' in the German Central European context, for individuals of Jewish descent did play a remarkably large role in both the German and Austrian Marxist Social Democratic movements. Marx was the most obvious case, and it is clear, even from his troubling 1844 essay, that the ideology of Jewish emancipation, in an odd dialectic, played a large role in his turning to dialectical materialism and the theory of rational, interest-based, class struggle. Yet Marx was only the most prominent in a whole cast of Jewish socialist intellectuals and leaders. Many of these, most notably the two leaders of Austrian Social Democracy, Victor Adler and then Otto Bauer, were the sons of successful capitalists. That the battle between capitalism and socialism in German Central Europe was so often fought out between Jewish capitalist fathers and Jewish socialist sons only served to encourage and confirm antisemitic suspicions of conspiracy, even when there was none.

Chapter 5
The perils of modernity

The 'irrationalist' critique of 'Jewish' modernity that informed so much of antisemitism was, as we have just seen, not quite as completely irrational as has often been claimed, and the circumstances of late 19th-century German Central Europe, the actual role played by Jews in the region's economy, politics, thought, and culture, made it all too credible. Yet there was also another, 'rational', even 'rationalist', side to antisemitism. The irony of the Jewish identification with rationalist modernity was that in Central and Eastern Europe there was ultimately nothing more threatening to Jews than the modernization of society – given the form of modernity in which that modernization took place.

Not all antisemitic ideologues of the late 19th century were irrationalist, objecting to the Jews because of their rationalism. One of the most influential antisemitic writers of the time, the economist, philosopher, and (anti-Marxist) socialist Eugen Dühring argued the reverse, that Jews were not rationalist enough, but rather were mystics, still blinded by atavistic superstition. It was because of their *lack* of rationality that Jews were unworthy of participating in progressive, scientific German society. Dühring's book from 1881, *The Jewish Question as a Racial, Moral and Cultural Problem*, was a key text in the development of a 'scientific' form of racial antisemitism. This used the prestige of Darwinian evolutionary biology to invert the debate about Jews and rationality. Many of the same arguments about Jewish blindness and superstition that went back to early Christianity were revisited and refashioned into 'scientific' theories about the inadequacy of the Jewish form of reasoning, as opposed to the higher, Christian or Aryan mode of truly rational thought.

Many of the stereotypes of the 'irrationalist' critique of Jews could be incorporated into this 'rationalist' assertion of the inadequate nature of the Jewish mind. Houston Stewart Chamberlain, the originally English son-in-law of Richard Wagner, combined 'irrationalist' Wagnerian cultural antisemitism with this new 'scientific' negative stereotype of Jews in his immensely successful *Foundations of the Nineteenth Century* from 1899. In this book, replete with the fashionable racial theorizing of the era, Chamberlain characterized Central European Jewry as spiritually backward and racial mongrels, who were not truly autonomous, rational beings. He made a Kantian distinction between Judaism as a heteronomous religion and Christianity as a religion of the internalized God, the true source of moral freedom. Jews used a lesser form of instrumental rationality and a materialist world view, as opposed to the Christian and Aryan reliance on belief and on authentic reason. While Jews followed a slave religion, Christian Aryans followed a religion of modern, free beings. Jewish rationality was, in this view, nothing but a lower, superficial form of reason, which informed such regressive and morally pernicious modes of thought as utilitarianism, 'destructive' capitalism, and Marxist (Jewish) socialism. It was up to Germans, and Aryans generally, to overcome this degenerate influence on Western civilization and return to the higher plane of thinking and scientific endeavour, as represented *in nuce* by the remarkable achievements of German culture, science, the German economy, and, above all, the German nation in the last decades of the 19th century. Aryan Germans represented the promise of a truly rational modernity, not materialistic Jews.

Chamberlain backed up his argument for a German modernity free of Jews, moreover, by using the most modern kind of scientific language: the language of Darwinian biology and its anthropological counterpart: race. Racial theory, and the distinction between 'Aryans' and 'Semites', pre-dated Darwin's *On the Origin of Species*, published in 1859. Benjamin Disraeli had written of Jews as a distinct and powerful race in his novel, *Coningsby*, of 1844. The French historian Ernest Renan had written of the distinction between the Aryan and Semitic races in 1848, and another Frenchman, secretary to Alexis de Tocqueville, Joseph Arthur de Gobineau, published the canonical text of racial theory, *Essay on the Inequality of the Human Races* between 1853 and 1855. Gobineau was not himself anti-Jewish. In his book he praised the Jews for their racial purity, although he thought the 'Aryan' race superior and disapproved of the mixing of races, and so was against the 'Semitization' of 'Aryan' Europeans. Nevertheless, Gobineau's work set the framework within which racial theory became a serious field of study. Moses Hess, famed as the precursor of Zionism for his *Rome and Jerusalem* of 1862, was an avid student of racial theory in the 1850s. The idea that behaviour and mentality were derived from natural, material transmission did, after all, fit very well into the materialism which was regarded at the time as the most modern philosophy.

Darwin's elegant proof of the (already posited) theory of evolution in 1859 simply confirmed and encouraged racial theories about human behaviour and character. It also greatly boosted the prestige attached to the biological model of enquiry, and undermined both the religious *and* the idealist interpretations of what human beings were. The idea of a Kantian uniform, equal 'kingdom of ends' all too easily made way for a view of humanity akin to the prevailing view of the animal kingdom, full of hierarchies of higher and lesser evolved species, in which only the fittest survived. The invidious consequences can be seen in the thinking of Herbert Spencer's Social Darwinism, on the one hand, but even worse in the racial thinking of the greatest avowed follower of Darwin in the world of German science, Ernst Haeckel, the founder of the monist movement. Haeckel, as with Gobineau, was not particularly anti-Jewish, but he clearly saw humanity in terms of a hierarchy of superior and inferior races, and the white Aryan race, particularly the Germans, was at the top, the 'Semitic' Jews inferior. His claim that 'politics is applied biology' summed up the racialist approach and completely undermined the rationalist framework on which Jewish emancipation and integration into Central European society had been based.

At the time, however, it was not at all clear that racialism was irrational or even anti-rationalist; indeed, it appeared to a great many to be solidly 'scientific' in its approach, and an enlightening, because materialist, replacement for the superstitions of religion and even that 'slave morality' so criticized by Nietzsche. The dubious nature of its claims to scientific status was evident to some at the time. The nomenclature of Aryan and Semite derived not from biology but from linguistics and its relevance to race relied on a shaky theory of ethnolinguistics. Chamberlain, one of the great champions of racial theory, could nevertheless see that there was little empirical proof for the 'science' of race and came to rely instead on proof of racial character by *subjective* feeling. Yet there were many academics, including many Jews, who took the categories of race seriously, and endeavoured to perform proper, scientific research on racial characteristics, involving such notorious techniques as cranial measurement, to investigate whether behaviour and mentality were indeed linked to genetically determined physiology.

The attempt to discover correlations between material biological, empirically verifiable qualities such as skin colour and head shape was, in its own way, an extension of the scientific, empirical method, no matter how bizarre and prejudiced its results appear to us today. One of the great founders of scientific criminology, Cesare Lombroso, was, as a materialist and hence biological determinist, convinced that criminals were born not made, and could be detected by their physical appearance. Lombroso, a Jew, was viewed as very progressive in his time for rejecting an 'unscientific', moralistic view of crime. Eugenics, the movement that sought to combat human 'degeneration' and racially improve humanity by proper breeding policies, was also seen at the turn of the 20th century as rational, progressive, scientific, and *modern*. George Bernard Shaw, *the* modern man of his age, was one of its greatest supporters.

It is also true that not all racial theories were innately antisemitic; indeed, some race scientists, many of them Jewish, saw 'Semites' as superior. Antisemitic racial theories were no more irrational than these philosemitic racial theories, or indeed any other racial theory, because the whole approach has been shown by modern science to be either completely chimeric, or, even in its postmodern guise of DNA decoding, quite marginal to other far more potent distinguishers in human behaviour and achievement, such as culture, environment, education, geography, and good fortune (and perhaps free will). Racially based theories such as eugenics have come to be discredited and viewed as either evil or totally misguided. Yet their 'unscientific' nature was not evident to a great many at the time.

It is, moreover, a comfortable illusion of our time to think that 'rationalist modernity' was only fitted to individualistic capitalism on the Western, liberal democratic model. Jeffrey Herf has pointed out that it was quite possible to have a 'reactionary modernism' in early 20th-century Germany, which attempted to use technological and scientific progress for illiberal and authoritarian ends. At the turn of the century, there was indeed a move away in the Western societies, including Britain, from the old 'Manchester' model of modernity, based on individual self-interest in the *laissez faire* free market, towards a much more collectivist model, in which the nation state, bureaucrats, and 'experts' played a far larger role in directing society and thus avoided the 'irrationalities' produced by individuals left to themselves. This could lead to a form of liberal reformism, as in Edwardian Britain, or in American Progressivism, but it could just as well lead to a form of modern authoritarian nationalism, and the country which exemplified this new, more corporatist form of modernity was Germany. The contrast between liberal Britain and authoritarian, machine-like Germany was a cliché of travel literature of the time, and Germany was seen as the more modern.

Within this framework, racial theory, and racial antisemitism, could appear as forms of what might be termed 'reactionary rationalism', for if it was scientifically shown that there were superior and inferior races, rationally, they should be treated accordingly, and if eugenics was proposing selective breeding to improve the national stock, then was not this logic also applicable to selectivity and discrimination between races? Such thinking, when applied to Jews, meant that antisemitism was not only the politics of cultural despair, or of the uneducated rabble, but also highly influential within (the non-Jewish part of) Germany and Austria's intellectual and academic elite.

Indeed, medical professors and students, with their bias in favour of the physiological, were particularly prominent among racial antisemitism's supporters. The supposed differences between the Aryan masculine ideal body type and its weaker, more effeminate Semitic counterpart – with its hooked nose, flat feet, round skull, and so forth – were seen to reflect spiritual, psychological difference. Jewish physicians, such as Sigmund Freud and Max Nordau, have been seen to be heavily affected by such thinking. Freud's tracing of the cause of antisemitism to the circumcision of Jewish men is probably linked to this sort of 'scientific' discourse about Jewish physiology. The supposed feminine nature of Jewish men was an especially prevalent theme, reflecting as it did the projected fears of non-Jewish men about the emancipation of their supposed gender and ethnic inferiors. Ironically, one of the canonical texts of this antisemitic literature, Otto Weininger's *Sex and Character*, while accepting the difference between 'Aryan' and

'Jewish' mentalities, and seeing this difference as similar to the polarity between 'Man' and 'Woman', did not equate 'Woman' with 'Jew'. Moreover, by making 'Jewishness' a spiritual and not a racial quality, Weininger (himself Jewish by descent) challenged the racially antisemitic assumptions of his day. By seeing 'Jewish' thought as collectivist and materialist as opposed to the 'Aryan's' individualism and idealism, Weininger asserted that antisemitism must therefore be 'Jewish'. Few beyond his Jewish readers noticed this dialectical counter-attack, however, and Weininger's supposed identification of Jews as immoral and feminine, and hence inferior, became part of racial antisemitism's ideological armoury.

The influence of racial theory was also closely bound up with the much increased prestige of nationalism in early 20th-century Europe. Even in multinational states, such as the Habsburg Monarchy, liberal parties either switched over to the more nationalist, often racially based form of self-identification, or were replaced by more radical nationalist parties. Among Austrian German Liberals, the criterion for inclusion in respectable society changed from being educated and 'rational' to being German, and while the latter could still be interpreted culturally, racial definitions became ever more popular, and antisemitic nationalist parties were eventually accepted as part of what had been the liberal, progressive Left in Austrian politics.

In Germany, the formation of a stronger national identity after 1871 was engineered by Bismarck through a process of 'negative integration' which identified Germans by defining who they were not. Hence Catholic Germans were initially identified in the *Kulturkampf* of the 1870s as questionable patriots, because of their allegiance to a foreign power (the Pope). Socialists were also identified as un-German and persecuted as such, as were the many Slavs within German territory, especially in the eastern, Polish sections of Prussia. Then, as Bismarck decided to switch from relying on liberal to conservative support around 1880, the

8. Adolf Stöcker (1835–1909). As founder of the Christian Social Party (1878) and the Berlin Movement (1881), Stöcker was the first major leader of political antisemitism in Germany.

antisemitic preaching of the court preacher, Adolf Stöcker, was allowed to proceed, and Bismarck gave his tacit backing to the idea that Jews also were not quite German. The exclusion of these groups from being part of the nation had the general effect of making them want even more to become a part of that nation, and it also cemented a sense of at least negative identity among those lucky enough not to be excluded.

Moreover, being a modern development, the new German nationalism demanded a uniformity of German identity and an exclusivity of national loyalty that differed markedly from traditional corporatist systems, which had allowed for diversity of identity and multiplicity of loyalties. It was an adaptation of a cornerstone of modern rationality, the logical rule of the excluded middle: one was *either* German, or one was of another national (racial) group. One could not be both; one could not, by this logic, owe allegiance to the Pope and be a real German; and one could not be loyal to a different ethnicity or religious group, such as the Jews, and still be a real German. This nationalist 'either/or' logic was quite 'rational', quintessentially 'rational', and an abhorrence for divided loyalties could be seen in the citizenship laws of many countries, including in American law, where loyalty to the United States *alone* was required.

As far as Central European Jews were concerned, this modern, rational demand for uniformity and univalence had always been the pressure behind the drive to integrate inherent in the emancipation movement, and the 'failure' of Jews to lose their difference had been a major reason for the survival of the 'Jewish Question'. This had, however, looked manageable and temporary, as Jews appeared well on the way to ever greater integration (assimilation) into German and Central European society. Once the definition of modernity had shifted to the more 'organic' and collectivist model, in which the 'reactionary rationalism' of biological thinking – and race – played such a large role, then Jewish difference became racially defined, and hence impossible to overcome. This tendency towards a racially based ethno-nationalism did not only affect Jewish status among Germans. It also compromised their integration in the eyes of many Czech, Polish, and Romanian nationalists, who had, being *modern* nationalists, adopted both the idea of individuals needing to have undivided loyalty to the national cause, and a 'scientific' quasi-racial definition of who was an 'authentic' member of the national family. The most significant case remained the German nationalist one, however, and it did not augur well for Jews that the most radical nationalist parties and organizations in both Germany and Austria before 1914, such as the Pan-German League, led by Heinrich Class, and the Austrian Pan-German Party, led by Georg von Schönerer, were racially antisemitic, the latter vehemently so.

Most Germans and Austrians, indeed even most German and Austrian-German nationalists, thought the extreme lengths to which figures such as Schönerer took their antisemitism to be unreasonable. Even if the prevalence of racial thinking and the logic of the nation state and nationalism pointed towards a racial antisemitic conclusion, there remained many other considerations and factors which prevented such a conclusion being either reached or acted upon by most people before 1914, indeed before 1933. Political antisemitism, it is worth pointing out, was only ever a small success in Imperial Germany and was by 1914 regarded as a failure. Even in Austria, where it was much more successful, antisemitism was kept in bounds by the (non-national) state. Antisemitic attitudes and practices had infiltrated German society, as they had Austria's various national societies even more successfully, but the radical, 'rational' consequences of racial antisemitism were not drawn, partly because older, non-rational political and moral values intervened to deem the 'rational' conclusions of racial theory as applied to Jews impractical, immoral, immoderate, and hence unreasonable.

Yet all too many Central and Eastern Europeans adopting antisemitic attitudes, or at least playing to them, did appear 'sensible', understood in terms of an instrumental rationality. The anti-Jewish hostility of Czech and Polish (and Ruthenian) nationalists within the Habsburg Monarchy was explicable in terms of the intricate ethnic and national balance within the Bohemian Crownlands and Galicia. In the Bohemian case, Jews had provided crucial votes to tip the balance in favour of German liberals against their Czech opponents, and they were often linguistically 'ambidextrous'. Not only did this go against the nationalist model of uniformity and univalence, but in more practical terms it meant that Jewish preference for the German cause had cost the Czech nationalists electoral success and hence power. Attacking Jews, and pressuring them to become 'Czech', at least in their political, national persona, thus had a real rationale, and the success of this pressure in the 'Czechization' of many Bohemian Jews after 1890 did enhance Czech power. Similarly, the hostility and pressure of the Polish-led authorities in Galicia against Galician Jewry succeeded in coercing a formal 'Polonization' of Jews, which had the effect of turning Galicia's population majority 'Polish' for the first time. The fact that Jews, perforce, now shored up Polish hegemony was in turn deeply resented by nationalist leaders of the Ruthenian 'minority'. Minority nationalist resentment against Jews in Hungary, from Romanians, Slovaks, and others, also had a real basis in the support of most Hungarian Jews for the Hungarian – Magyar – national cause. Jews in these cases were, for whatever reason, supporting the national enemy, or at least not supporting 'us', and in the 'us versus them' world of modern nationalism that was all that mattered.

In Eastern Europe, especially in Russia, complex considerations of minority nationalisms also played a role. Roman Dmowski, leader of the Polish National Democrats, launched an economic boycott of Jews partially to shore up Polish national identity in Russia. The

Kishinev pogrom of 1903, against the myth, was not instigated by the Tsarist authorities; rather, it was provoked by a Russian nationalist and extremely antisemitic newspaper editor, A. P. Krushevan, in a city where ethnic Russians were a small minority and Jews and Romanian-speaking Moldavians were the major groups. The Tsarist Interior Minister at the time, however, Viacheslav Plehve, was, as with most Tsarist officials, hostile to Jews and had fostered the sort of political climate where extremist reactionaries such as Krushevan were allowed to function, because it kept Jews and their liberal and progressive allies off-balance, and divided and distracted the opposition.

In Central Europe, scapegoating of Jews was also used as a favourite political device by many politicians, most famously Karl Lueger, founder of the Christian Social Party in Austria, and mayor of Vienna 1897–1910. Much of Lueger's success was due to his mastery of the new, mass 'modern' politics that emerged as a consequence of modernization and the expansion of the franchise in most Western countries in the late 19th century. The new politics followed the change in the character of 'modernity' discussed above, in that it was much more corporatist and collectivist in its approach than the preceding, liberal era of 'honorary' politics. Instead of politics being a process decided between individual politicians, it became far more a matter of party machines, with divisions more explicitly along class and ethnic lines. Lueger's genius was to realize that in Vienna the most effective means to assemble a political coalition to challenge and defeat the Liberal hegemony over Vienna's municipal politics was to identify 'them', the image of the political enemy, not as 'liberal' but as 'Jewish', in a classic, if hypertrophic, example of the sort of ethnic tactics often used in modern Western urban politics.

Yet Lueger would not have been successful in this tactic were antisemitic hostility not widespread in Vienna, cutting across lines of ideology and interest, and if this had not been combined with the real social and economic situation of Central European Jewry,

Schaue ich aus, als ob ich ein Juden-
fresser wäre?

9. 'Do I look like I would eat Jews?', *Glühlichter*, December 1892. Karl
Lueger (1844–1910), Austrian Christian Social leader and mayor of
Vienna, was notorious for his cynical opportunism and hypocrisy
regarding antisemitism; he was one of Hitler's role models, together
with Georg von Schönerer, in *Mein Kampf*.

especially in Vienna. The fact is that Central European Jews had indeed done remarkably well in the modern, capitalist economy, and many of the more successful, and most successful, had settled in Vienna. There were many poor Jews in Vienna, but there was also a coterie of extremely wealthy Jewish banking, commercial, and industrial 'dynasties' and alongside this a substantial prosperous business and professional middle class. By the turn of the century, Jews really did control many, if not most, of Austria's major banks, much of the textile industry and the coal and steel industry was run by Jews or individuals of Jewish descent, such as Karl Wittgenstein, Ludwig's father, and many of Vienna's most prominent retail stores were also 'in Jewish hands'. Roughly half of all lawyers and physicians in Vienna were Jewish, and a large majority of the editorial staff of the city's most prestigious newspaper, the *Neue Freie Presse*, was Jewish. The culture of *Vienna 1900* was not entirely a creation of Jews, but Jews were predominant, especially in such fields as literature, psychoanalysis, philosophy, and progressive economic, legal, and political thought.

When Jewish material success had first become particularly evident, in the 1860s, it was generally accepted by the authorities and populace, because these were the prosperous 'founders' years' of rapid economic growth. Behind Jewish acceptance was an implicit bargain: the assumption was that liberal economic policies, which enabled Jews to achieve their new status of prosperity, would also provide for the prosperity of non-Jews. Any latent resentment at a formerly oppressed, pariah group suddenly leapfrogging most of the populace to be both materially more successful and socially superior was kept in check by the rational calculation that everyone could gain from the new dispensation.

This began to change radically in 1873. The economic good times came to an end with the Crash of 9 May, when a run on the Viennese Stock Exchange spread to the financial centres of the rest of Europe and ushered in the long era of the (19th-century) Depression. The damage done by the Crash was more psychological than material. The economy recovered relatively quickly and the late 19th century was an era of remarkable technological progress. The Crash had, however, destroyed the populace's faith in *laissez faire* economics, and the political liberalism that went with it, and the compromising of liberalism also had a negative influence on the standing in public opinion of its allies in Central European Jewry. There was a time lag between the Crash and political liberalism's decline in both Germany and Austria, but it is striking that the end of liberal hegemony in Central Europe around 1879 was followed almost immediately by the emergence of political antisemitism.

There was a certain rational calculus that could explain this: Jews, viewed as a separate group, had been acceptable and welcome as entrepreneurs and 'money-people' who knew how to create prosperity. That is how they continued to be welcomed in Hungary as allies of the Magyar national cause. In Vienna, however, once the economic circumstances had tightened, and Jews, unlike those in the non-Jewish middle and lower middle classes, still appeared to have kept most of their gains, and even be increasing them, attitudes darkened. As long as Jews were still viewed as not 'one of us', as a competing ethnic group, who had been allowed to rise from their divinely ordained state of wretchedness to become full members of society precisely in order to help make the pie bigger for all, then it seemed reasonable to see their economic gains as a slice of the pie which should, by rights, be 'ours'.

Much of German Central European antisemitism can thus be seen as an extreme attempt at wealth redistribution, on ethnic rather than class lines. Those on the democratic and socialist Left have concurred with the Viennese Democrat Ferdinand Kronawetter that antisemitism in this economic sense was an irrational 'socialism of fools'. Yet in some circumstances, especially in Vienna, the rationale does not look that insane – evil, cynical, and selfish, but instrumentally rational. If Jewish pedlars were providing goods at lower prices than their non-Jewish shopkeeper equivalents, then banning the Jewish competition made (short-term) sense. If graduating Jewish medical students were competing in very large numbers for academic and professional appointments, then it made sense, for non-Jewish counterparts, to seek a *numerus clausus* to reduce Jewish competition. If Jewish student activists had been so central to the birth of radical, socially oriented German nationalist student politics that they occupied many leadership positions in the movement (as they did in the late 1870s), then it was 'rational' for non-Jewish rivals to insist that the movement be true to its national purity and dismiss those Jews on the grounds of racial antisemitism.

Once Jews were seen as 'them', then the dynamics of ethnic politics often meant that the 'rational', even 'modern' answer was to target the Jewish 'out group' as the source of compensation for the 'compact majority'. The fact that such a large proportion of Vienna's populace was not Austrian German but rather Czech, Slovak, or some other ethnicity only reinforced the attraction of this manoeuvre, because by identifying Jews as the 'foreigner', all the other groups could become 'Viennese' in a massive exercise in 'negative integration'. In the long term this antisemitic form of resource redistribution was indeed a 'socialism of fools', if only because Jewish individuals were very productive members of the economy and society. But then many would argue that *socialism* is a 'socialism of fools' for the same reason – that it sacrifices long-term growth for short-term gains. In the Viennese example, there were actually quite a few short- and medium-term gains for non-Jews who had either adopted Lueger's antisemitic message or voted for it. Christian Socials, after all, became the party in power, and indeed became the main conservative, bourgeois party in Austria; and Lueger's municipalization of utilities in Vienna, which he sold in antisemitic terms as rescuing the people's resources from the 'Jewish' capitalists – and financed with credit from banks run by Jews – is to this day regarded as a triumph of municipal governance.

This corporatist version of modernity, which saw society in terms of 'natural' wholes and groups rather than as individual rational actors, when interlaced with the division between a Jewish 'them' and a non-Jewish 'us' was ultimately extremely dangerous. Yet this result of 'modernity' was far from an inevitable aspect of all modernity. Its corporatist, holistic character was not shared by the predominant form of modernity in the English-speaking world and Western Europe. Countries such as Britain, the United States, and France, as mentioned above, were also influenced in a more collectivist, corporatist direction, but nowhere near to the same extent, and there was a strong, liberal democratic, individualist and pluralist counter-current. It was not 'modernity' as such, but a particular, Central European kind that was most liable to this antisemitic temptation. Even then, it only succumbed to that temptation in particular circumstances, when combined with the factors outlined in previous chapters. When this combination did occur, however, it did so with horrendous consequences.

Chapter 6
Concatenations

The building blocks of antisemitism outlined in previous chapters had all been assembled by 1914. Racial antisemitism and ethno-nationalism had blocked the prospect of a full integration of Jews into Central and Eastern European society, asserting Jewish racial inferiority and excluding them from the national community. Religious antisemitism, recapitulating Christian anti-Judaism, eyed Jews as following a superficial and materialistic religion for blind unbelievers. Economic antisemitism, based on fear and envy at the supposed stranglehold of 'the Jews' over finance, accused Jews of being behind the depredations of capitalism on the traditional economy. Cultural antisemitism saw materialistic, abstract Jewish rationalism as responsible for the disenchantment of the world through the 'rule of Mammon' (the money-based economy) and Marxist socialism, to say nothing of Freudian psychoanalysis's reduction of the irrational world of the unconscious to a series of sordid sexual problems. Even the over-arching principle of the international Jewish world conspiracy was available. The *Protocols of the Elders of Zion*, a fairly obvious forgery, probably cooked up around 1902 by members of the Russian secret service and based on various 19th-century works of fiction, set out the elements of a Jewish plan to use capitalism and socialism to set the non-Jews against each other and hence conquer the world. The *Protocols* were not actually available to anything but a Russian audience until after the First World War, but in any case Western and Central European antisemites, going back at least to Wilhelm Marr's *Victory of Jewry over Germandom* from 1879, had already made more or less the same claim about Jews internationally conspiring to wreak their revenge on Gentile society.

Yet, for all of this, Western and Central European Jewry still enjoyed equal rights with their non-Jewish fellow citizens, most enjoyed increasing prosperity, and the integration of Jews into society and culture proceeded, with Jewish individuals having an ever larger role in European modern culture. The various forms of antisemitism might have established themselves by 1914, but only in particular contexts, such as Vienna and German Austria, the Bohemia Crownlands, Galicia, and a few more rural parts of Germany, in Hesse and Saxony, had political antisemitism achieved success – and even that was on the wane. Even in Russia, the Jewish community had become much more assertive against the oppressive Tsarist state, and Jews could look forward with some confidence to a brighter future, either as a result of progressive reform, or socialist revolution, with both Russian progressive liberals and socialists supporting full Jewish emancipation. The ritual murder trial of Menahem Beilis in 1913, although a reminder of Russian atavism, resulted in Beilis's acquittal, and saw many Russian intellectuals criticize the antisemitic machinations of the Tsarist authorities.

The emergence of antisemitism in all its various forms had, admittedly, profoundly affected the Jewish situation within European society. Even in Britain and the United States, the large flow of Jewish immigrants around the turn of the century fleeing persecution and penury in Russia was met by a social and cultural animosity in some circles in which the usual nativist reaction to immigrants was tinged, or worse, with antisemitism. The British 'Aliens Act' of 1905 restricting immigration was aimed mainly at

Eastern European Jews. France and French Jewry were still recovering from the trauma of the Dreyfus Affair. In Austria, the antisemitic Christian Socials, combining religious and economic antisemitism, dominated the municipal government of Vienna and were the major clerical-conservative force in German Austria; and racial antisemitism, especially among the formerly liberal non-Jewish part of the intelligentsia, had added to Jews, especially in Vienna, being both politically alienated and socially isolated. Similarly in Germany, antisemitic attitudes had spread into many political and social organizations, especially on the more right-wing, conservative side, leaving the more astute or sensitive among German Jews concerned at the implications for the project of full integration. Informal bans on Jews in various parts of both the German and Austrian state and even academia persisted. In the Prussian officer corps, a ban on individuals of Jewish descent was upheld. Antisemitism put paid to the idea of the 'disappearance' of Jews into German and Austrian society. One of the consequences of this adoption by mainstream politics of antisemitic attitudes and behaviours, however, was that the movement of political antisemitism, threatening around 1880, and again around 1893, had petered out in Germany by 1914. Even in Austria, the Christian Socials had only implemented minor, harassing measures against Jews, and in any case were prevented from serious persecution by the state authorities' upholding of the equal rights of Jewish citizens, as was the case also in the German Empire and its various states. The highpoint of *political* antisemitism appeared to have passed by 1914.

Central European Jews, similar to their Eastern European counterparts, had, moreover, adjusted to this new situation. One response to the rise of racism and ethno-nationalism had been to adopt the same approach to their own identity: the Zionism of Theodor Herzl both accepted the assertion that Jews were indeed a foreign 'people' and criticisms that Jews were suffering from a moral crisis. Hence his 'modern solution' to the Jewish Question was that the Jews should go off and found a separate, modern state of their own, to improve themselves, cure European society of antisemitism, *and* complete the emancipation by integration into humankind, but as a nation rather than as individuals. By 1914, this effort had not achieved much concretely, but had received the moral support of the German, British, and even Russian governments. Other Zionists, such as Richard Beer-Hofmann, were less enthusiastic about a political solution, but saw the assertion of an ethnocultural Jewish identity as a moral act. Even many of those Jews still committed to full integration into German and Austrian society at large took a more assertive approach, resulting in the formation of self-defence organizations such as the *Centralverein* (Central Association of Germans of the Jewish Faith) in Germany and the *Österreichisch-israelitische Union* (Austrian-Israelitic Union). Other Central European Jews, disillusioned by political liberalism's weakness and readiness to compromise with antisemitic nationalists, transferred their support to socialism, seeing this as the last major political movement to preserve the Enlightenment's ideal of an equal humanity. Yet others, probably the majority, simply continued to go about their business, convinced that progress would eventually overcome the irritant of antisemitism, which appeared quite a reasonable view in 1914, despite everything. For all of antisemitism's prevalence, it had not by any means coalesced into the horrific juggernaut it became.

How did this apparently manageable situation result in the Holocaust?

The short answer is that 1914 saw the beginning of what has been called the 'general crisis and Thirty Years War of the 20th century', which culminated in the genocidal crimes and ultimate defeat of Hitler's Third Reich. It is only in the light of the collapse and traumatization of European civilization in the First World War, the emergence of Bolshevik Russia, and the subsequent failure to restore 'normalcy' in Europe and the global economy, that Hitler's ability to become *Führer* (which just means leader) of Germany and bring about the realization of his dreams of exterminating the Jews can be explained. Recognizing this, however, is only a beginning, for the ways in which antisemitism did and did not contribute to this tragic course of events necessitates a much longer, more complex answer.

To start with, the First World War initially brought an improvement of the Jewish situation in Central Europe. The need for national solidarity of all the main combatant states produced in Germany a 'civic peace', in which Emperor William II claimed to 'know no parties any more, I know only Germans', and Jews were included within this broad definition of German identity. Many Russian Jews viewed the German troops who conquered their area of Russia as liberators. In Austria-Hungary a similar rallying to the supranational Monarchy occurred, in which ethnic hostilities, including antisemitism, were, momentarily, suspended. Jews in both Germany and the Monarchy made crucial contributions to the war effort, most famously Walther Rathenau's organization of Germany's war economy.

Soon enough, however, as the hopes of quick victory faded, the war dragged on, and became ever more destructive of resources and manpower, the initial sentiment of patriotic solidarity gave way to a more suspicious, divisive, and authoritarian nationalism, in which old prejudices about Jews as parasitic aliens, a state within a state, flourished once more. In 1916, the Prussian war minister instituted a 'Jew census' to ascertain whether accusations by antisemitic politicians of Jewish shirking from war sacrifice were merited, signalling to German Jewry that the hopes for full acceptance by the Prussian establishment were dashed.

The early territorial losses of the Central Powers on the Eastern Front also created large migration streams of East European Jews (*Ostjuden*) to Germany, Prague, and particularly Galicians to Vienna. These more traditionalist Jews, less acculturated to German Central European culture, represented a direct challenge, in their evident difference, to German Jewish claims to complete assimilation. Antisemites could now point to 'real' Jews, and assert that their Western counterparts were, for all their apparently civilized manner, just the same under the sophisticated veneer. Moreover, assimilated Jews were torn between distaste for what they viewed as their poor, scruffy, uneducated, and unenlightened co-religionists, and feelings of pity for their plight and solidarity for their fellow Jews. The presence of the Jewish refugees in the Central European capitals had the net effect of reminding Jews of their Jewish roots, but also of encouraging and confirming racial and cultural antisemitic stereotypes. In April 1918, Prussia banned Jewish migration, arguing explicitly that the Jewish migrants were 'work-shy, unclean, morally unreliable ... to a great extent infested with lice ... especially apt carriers and spreaders of typhus and other infectious diseases.' Galician refugees in Vienna produced the same sort of reaction by the Christian Social municipal administration, which was only prevented from seriously antisemitic measures, such as a threatened expulsion, by the Habsburg authorities. The waning days of the Central Powers, as they faced economic crisis, social catastrophe, military defeat, and political destruction, saw a return to antisemitic policies and attitudes that pointed both backwards to pre-emancipation 'Jew laws' and forwards to the Nazis.

The leadership in Berlin also attempted to make Jews the direct scapegoats for defeat. When all was lost in November 1918, Erich Ludendorff tried to get Albert Ballin, the Jewish shipping magnate and ardent German patriot, to head the government and thus make a Jew responsible for accepting defeat. Ballin only avoided this fate by committing suicide. With no factual basis, the Jews nevertheless became heavily implicated in the 'stab in the back myth' by which the German Right explained their military failure after the war.' This was partly because influential Jewish bankers and industrialists had indeed been pressing for a more moderate, pragmatic war policy since near the war's beginning, and hence were regarded as 'defeatist' by the hard Right. Partly too, Jews became very prominent on the Left in both German and Austrian politics. When the Central Powers' war effort collapsed in late 1918, and revolutions broke out in Germany and in the Habsburg Monarchy, individuals of Jewish descent (Jews as far as most Europeans were concerned) were to be found in many leading positions in those revolutions, as they had been in the Bolshevik Revolution in November 1917 in Russia. The wave of socialist or communist revolutions after 1918 subsided after a few years, except in the Soviet Union, but the list of Jewish revolutionaries – Eisner, Landauer, Luxemburg, Kun, Lukacs, Trotsky, and many others – served to confirm antisemitic assertions about what now became the threat of 'Judaeo-Bolshevism'.

Moreover, the immediate postwar governments that succeeded the imperial regimes in Germany and Austria, and of necessity had to accept the Versailles Peace settlement, had large contingents of the liberal and moderate socialist Left, and hence many of the leading political figures in both Germany and Austria were Jewish. Hugo Preuss was instrumental in setting up the Weimar Republic, and Carl Melchior was heavily involved in negotiating the financial terms of the Peace. Rathenau was a central figure of the immediate postwar government and in 1922 became Foreign Minister, with a policy of fulfilment (and renegotiation) of Versailles' terms. His assassination in 1922 was one of the leading early 'triumphs' of interwar antisemitism. In Austria, the Foreign Minister at the end of the war was Victor Adler, and his successor (also as leader of the Austrian Social Democratic Party) Otto Bauer. It was thus easy, if quite unjustified, for antisemites to blame Jews for the surrender to the Western Allies.

The First World War might have officially ended on 11 November 1918, but in Central and Eastern Europe war just gave way to a general, most traumatic political, economic, and social crisis. Revolution and civil war seemed for a few years ubiquitous and never-ending, with the Bolshevik leadership of the new Soviet Union still hoping to spread the 'permanent revolution' to the states to its west, and the Western allies trying to destroy the 'Red menace'. Hence war between the new Poland and the Soviet Union went on into 1921, and fear at the spread of Bolshevism added severity to the suppression of the Spartakist revolution in Berlin, the Bavarian Soviet Republic in Munich, and the Hungarian Soviet Republic in Budapest in 1919. At the same time, the severe economic dislocation caused by the war was only made worse by the redrawing of borders in the peace settlement. Exacerbated by the political infighting over the peace, hyperinflation seized most of the Central European economies into the early 1920s, most famously and surreally in Weimar Germany, destroying much of the economic base of the bourgeoisie. The combination of radical insecurity and national humiliation for the losers, and national jubilation for the small-nation winners, created a most unstable and potent brew in which antisemitism often accompanied authoritarian reaction and the assertion of national power.

In the Soviet Union itself, Jews initially benefited from the recognition of the equality of all citizens, but then again Jews as members of a religious community also became the targets of Bolshevist atheism. In Poland and Czechoslovakia, Jews were accused of being allies of the national enemy, and hence became the targets of pogroms and riots. In Hungary, the 'White Terror' of the forces of Admiral Horthy ushered in a much more hostile attitude to Jews. In Romania, despite the official emancipation of 1919, the government remained hostile and discriminatory towards Jews. In Western Europe as well, the apparent link between Jews and Bolshevism caused otherwise sane politicians, such as Winston Churchill in 1920, to see Bolshevism as the product of internationalist Jewish atheists; the cogency of the antisemitic picture of the Jewish threat behind the wrenching upheaval was increased when Russian reactionaries, fleeing the Bolsheviks, brought editions of the *Protocols* to the West. These were then translated and published, most notoriously by Henry Ford's *Dearborn Independent* in instalments between 1920 and 1922. In Germany, antisemitic demagogues railed against the peace settlement, the economic disaster of inflation and the speculation that accompanied it, as well as the 'degenerate' modern culture that had developed as a response to and reflection of the chaotic times, and denounced it all as 'Jewish'. One such demagogue, Adolf Hitler, organized a revolt in Munich, the Beer

10. Henry Ford (1863–1947). The great American industrialist was also one of the most prominent American antisemites. In instalments in his *The Dearborn Independent* between 1920 and 1922, Ford introduced *The Protocols of the Elders of Zion* to the American public.

Hall Putsch of November 1923, to end this 'Jewish' oppression of the Germans, and Winifred Wagner, daughter-in-law of Richard, marched in his crowd of supporters.

Yet the 1923 Putsch was a fiasco that was quickly put down, and once economic and political order was restored in Germany and Austria, the second half of the 1920s was one of the best periods for German Central European Jews. Both Berlin and Vienna, the two cities with by far the largest Jewish populations in the region, were ruled by socialist administrations which ensured Jews equal rights and opportunities. Jews gained academic positions at a rate much higher than before the war, and their civic equality appeared assured by the German and Austrian constitutions. Even if antisemitic attitudes on the Right and in the bastions of the old establishment and non-Jewish intelligentsia festered, and antisemitic incidents in daily life continued, it looked as though the worst was over, and a tolerable normalcy established. Weimar Berlin and Red Vienna were highpoints in the Jewish participation in modern thought and culture, and this was also an era in which many Jews reasserted a more overt Jewish identity, often in association with the Jewish nationalist movement of Zionism.

In Czechoslovakia as well, the situation markedly improved after 1920, with the Czech political leadership under Thomas Masaryk making an effort to rein in the antisemitic tendencies of Czech nationalism. For the rest of the interwar period, Czechoslovakia was a model of tolerance and acceptance concerning Jews. In stark contrast, Hungary, previously the most hospitable land in Central Europe for Jews, became in 1920 the first to impose antisemitic discriminatory legislation, in the form of a *numerus clausus* law restricting the numbers of Jewish students at university. This abrupt change in approach was partly because of the fact that the 'liberal' pre-war political leadership had been replaced by the reactionary, authoritarian regime of Admiral Horthy, who saw Jews as untrustworthy and the allies of 'Jewish' communism, as demonstrated by the number of Jews in the communist revolutionary government of 1919. There were also more rational considerations, however: as Hungary had lost its nationality battle in 1918–19, losing two-thirds of its territory and almost all its minority population, there was no longer any need for Jews as allies in that conflict, and educated Jews now stood in the way, or were 'unfair' competition, for the scions of the Magyar gentry who now required clerical or salaried jobs in the dislocated economy. The fact that discrimination took place specifically on entry to the university speaks to the 'rational' aspect of ethnic interest in Hungarian antisemitism.

In Poland as well, where Jews had never been as integrated as they had been in Hungary or German Central Europe, the government continued through the 1920s to discriminate against Jews in state employment and economic policies, and the Polish universities instituted an informal *numerus clausus* when an official one failed to pass in 1923. Romania was similarly hostile to Jews, especially those acquired from Hungary in 1918–19. In the new 'nation states' of East Central Europe, with the Czech exception, the logic of ethno-nationalism meant that Jews, despite being 'citizens' on paper, were regarded as not of the national group, as aliens, and hence not deserving of benefiting from the nation's common wealth. At the beginning of 1930, the situation of Jews in Germany and Austria, by comparison, looked relatively good.

A bare three years later, Hitler's coming to power dramatically changed this, as did the Austro-fascist takeover in Austria in the same year, if to a lesser extent. The reason for this was that the hoped-for 'normalcy' of the mid-1920s proved all too brief, destroyed by the economic recession that started in Germany in 1927, and then became a slump after the Wall Street Crash in 1929, and a catastrophe after the Central European financial collapse of 1931. The main beneficiary of the economic and political crisis that was unleashed was Hitler and his National Socialist Party. The party's radical antisemitism had very little to do with its devastating electoral and political success in Germany after 1928. Instead, the major cause of Nazi success was the abject failure of the established political parties in Germany to find a solution to Germany's economic woes, the impatience of what remained of the old Prussian military establishment with constitutional procedures, and the succumbing of the conservative elite around President Hindenburg to the tempting illusion that they could exploit Hitler's popularity to restore a more authoritarian, conservative, but not radically fascist, settlement on Weimar Germany.

It seems clear that the portion of the German electorate that voted for the Nazis did so mostly as a desperate reaction to economic disaster and political inertia, which was in effect a collapse of modernity itself. In 1928, the Nazis had only 2% of the national vote; in 1930, 17%; 1932, 37%; reaching a high point in the election of March 1933 with 44%. (Even with his hands on the reins of power, Hitler never gained an absolute majority for his party alone.) It was Hitler's charismatic promise that he could, by his will, provide salvation for the country by a nationalist form of collectivist, 'socialist' policies, where republican, democratic Weimar had failed, that won him and his party votes. This was combined with an effective party organization, a sophisticated political aesthetic based on Wagnerian principles, and a ruthless employment of the culture of violence learned in the trenches, to produce the strongest nationalist political organization yet seen in Germany. Even so, it took the calculating acquiescence of the governing circles to allow Hitler into power, and, after the seizure of power, the continuing readiness of the state's servants to obey the Nazi regime's 'legal' orders destroying the constitution and many measures protective of basic civic rights, for Hitler to parlay his electoral effectiveness into actual power. Throughout this period in which Hitler came to power, when Hitler was attempting to prove his respectability, the party's antisemitism was de-emphasized, because it was seen as a political liability in public opinion. Only after the passage of the Enabling Act of 23 March 1933, when the Nazis gained total power, did they reveal the full scope of their political extremism, and of their antisemitism.

The roots of that extreme antisemitism, and of the party's national socialist ideology, have been traced back to the old Austria, to Vienna, where Hitler spent a miserable few years as a teenager, and to German Bohemia, where German nationalist ideologues attempted to attract the lower classes with a concept of nationally based social welfare and policy. Hitler moved to Munich in 1913 and joined the German Army during the war, in which he was severely wounded and traumatized. Back in Munich after the war, he became a street orator, spewing the sort of extreme nationalist and racial antisemitic rhetoric that had already interested him in Vienna. By 1923, he was leader of the German National Socialists in Munich and staged the abortive Beer Hall Putsch. Given a lenient sentence typical for right-wing radicals under the conservative court system, Hitler wrote *Mein Kampf* in Landsberg prison, making clear his extreme antisemitism, and became the darling of the radical Right. Once out of prison, he resumed leadership of the party and led its reorganization. Yet it was only with the crisis of the late 1920s that he became a serious figure in German politics, and only in 1933, with the seizure of power, that the full implications of his National Socialist agenda became evident.

11. 'The Eternal Jew', Nazi poster (1937). Jewish world conspiracy: 'The Jew' has money in one hand, a whip (power) in the other, and the Soviet Union in his pocket.

Chapter 7
Consequences

Once in power, Hitler and the Nazi leadership quickly dismantled all political institutions in Germany apart from their own, and clamped down hard on any opposition. They also tried to implement their antisemitic policies, instituting an economic boycott on 1 April 1933, but this initial foray was a failure and was called off after a day. Indeed, in the initial phase of Nazi rule, Jewish life in Germany was not impossible, because of Nazi wariness about international and domestic public opinion, and the piecemeal nature of their anti-Jewish policy. Even when racism was institutionalized with the Nuremberg laws of 1935, there was little physical violence against Jews and many German Jews assumed that the regime would become more moderate with time, an assumption which the easing of persecution during the Berlin Olympics encouraged. Hitler was also careful to rein in his worst antisemitic rhetoric in public speeches. Meanwhile, discriminatory legislation and policy against Jews, including the 'Aryanization' (legalized theft) of Jewish property, gradually increased, leading to ever greater segregation of Jews from other Germans.

The first major mass violence aimed at Jews in German Central Europe only occurred in March 1938, not in Germany but in newly 'annexed' Austria, and it was not orchestrated by the German Nazi regime but rather was spontaneous. Austria, especially Vienna, home of Lueger's Christian Socials, had a tradition of being an especially strong centre of antisemitism. During the era of socialist control of Vienna, the capital city was seen as a haven for Jews, but the rise of the 'Austro-fascist' regime of Engelbert Dollfuss and Kurt Schuschnigg in the 1930s saw a return of antisemitic discrimination by the state, at least informally. At the same time, Austro-fascism was aimed at preserving a conservative Catholic hegemony in Austria against both socialists *and* Nazis. When Hitler called the international community's bluff in March 1938 and invaded Austria, the resulting *Anschluss* (union) was greeted with much joy by a large proportion of the Austrian populace, and many seized the opportunity of attacking and humiliating, and also robbing, Jews as part of the celebration of 'national unity'.

The violence against Jews in Vienna in March was a precedent for the more widespread violence against Jews throughout the Third Reich (and also in Vienna) of 9–10 November 1938, *Reichskristallnacht*, which saw many shops and synagogues burned and many Jews attacked and even killed. In Germany, it appears that Nazi antisemitic policies were not particularly popular, and had to be carefully calibrated in the early years to match public acceptance. The Nazi authorities were quite sensitive to public opinion, and responded to public disquiet over Nazi policy towards the Catholic Church, for instance, by moderating policy. Similarly, after the initial failure of the economic boycott in April 1933, Nazi policy on Jews was ratcheted up gradually with one eye to public reactions. The fact that the authorities nevertheless continued increasing the level of persecution of Jews indicates both the centrality of antisemitism to Nazi ideology, but also the relative apathy with which non-Jewish Germans regarded the fate of their Jewish fellow citizens. There was simply not the same degree of outrage and resistance that there was on other issues.

Many Germans might not have approved of the severe antisemitic policies pursued by the Nazis, but their disquiet never rose to the level that would overcome their fear of Nazi retaliation and obedience to the dictates of the state-sanctioned regime, even if it was in the hands of radical, racist extremists. Jews, after all, were still seen as different, not 'one of us', and associated with the failed modernity of Weimar. If many of Germany's foremost intellectuals and artists were prepared to tolerate Nazi policy, also towards the Jews, and if eminent philosophers such as Martin Heidegger could see in Nazism a new, vital combination of thought and action that superseded the old, mechanistic ideas of democracy and individual civic rights, then why should ordinary Germans question the new regime, when it did not immediately affect them or their dearest values? For most of Germany, it was not active antisemitism on the part of the populace that was behind Nazi persecution of Jews, but rather a lack of sufficient resistance to that persecution: Nazi antisemitic policies proceeded by default. What Arendt called the 'banality of evil' of the death camps was preceded and enabled by the 'evil of banality' of most Germans' apathy towards the fate of German Jews.

The experience in Vienna appears to have been different. Here, in 1938, the city with by far the largest Jewish population in the Third Reich, there was a strong antisemitic undercurrent among a large part of the populace. Even in 1938, despite the discriminatory policies of Austro-fascism, Jews still owned many properties, ran many businesses, and were in many academic and professional positions. All of this, from a perspective of instrumentally rational antisemitism, might be transferred to deserving (covetous) non-Jews. Local Nazis took the initiative on Jewish policy, presaging and influencing, it has been argued, the policies at the centre that would lead to the Final Solution. The central issue, after the spate of 'wild Aryanization' that accompanied the events of March 1938, was Vienna's chronic housing crisis. In Germany proper, Jews up until 1938 had largely been left their housing; in Vienna, Jews occupied 60,000 housing units, and soon after March local pressure built to solve the housing shortage by evicting Jews from their apartments, concentrating them in fewer and less desirable units. Then a further step was proposed to free up more space: building a concentration camp for Jews outside the city. Before this could be built, circumstances changed and another solution was proposed and implemented: shipping Jews to occupied Poland. In its own terms, this ethnic form of social policy was quite sensible, even if it was morally heinous.

Nazi policy towards the Jewish Problem had a very pragmatic side. Given their antisemitic contention that Jews were not German and therefore should not be part of German society, but recognizing the limits on their actions set by domestic and international standards, the initial Nazi policy was to encourage Jews to leave Germany, and to facilitate this both by rank intimidation and persecution at home, and improving emigrants' prospects abroad. Hence the Nazi regime made a 'devil's pact' with Zionists in the Ha'avara Agreement which allowed German Jews

12. Jews scrubbing the street in Vienna, March 1938

to realize at least part of their assets when emigrating in return for the purchase of German export goods in Palestine. Adolf Eichmann's job in Vienna after March 1938 was devoted to forcing Jews to emigrate, while fleecing them of as much of their property as possible. Had the Evian Conference of July 1938 been more successful in opening up Western immigration quotas for German Jews, the likelihood is that the Nazis would have happily permitted Jews to leave. One of the reasons, however, why Evian failed was that Western governments were concerned that the antisemitic governments that ruled in much of Eastern Europe, including Poland, Hungary, and Romania, would want to take this opportunity to force their (much larger) Jewish populations out as well. Part of the Jewish tragedy in the 1930s was that almost all countries, even those in the West, were so pressed by social and economic distress that principles of equality and human rights were sidelined when it came to Central and Eastern European Jews – for they were regarded as 'foreign' not only in the lands of their potential emigration, but also in their own countries.

When war was declared in 1939, and Germany conquered Poland in short order, Nazi policy changed again. Germany now had a hugely greater number of Jews to deal with, and much more space, away from domestic and international attention, in which to operate. Much of the Polish populace was positively antisemitic, and much of the rest was largely indifferent to the fate of the Jews, whom they did not regard, generally, as part of the Polish nation. Nazi authorities, perhaps inspired by Viennese precedent, could therefore start realizing a much more brutally antisemitic policy of ghettoization of Polish Jews, and transport of Jews from Germany and other occupied countries to the Polish ghettoes. By the summer of 1941, with the heady success of the Third Reich's armies on all sides (except for Britain), it appeared that Hitler could realize his dearest dream and conquer Soviet Russia. As part of that campaign, he would also want to eradicate not only communists, but what he viewed as the allies of Bolshevism, Russian Jewry. SS 'task force' units (*Einsatzgruppen*), which accompanied the German forces in the invasion of Russia in 1941, soon set about the mass killing of Jewish communities. Hence, long before the Wannsee Conference of 20 January 1942, the eradication of the Jewish 'enemy' was a prime aim of Hitler's policy. Wannsee merely reiterated this for the rest of the Nazi bureaucracy, and sought more effective means, using industrial methods and new technologies, to realize the 'Final Solution' to the 'Jewish Problem', in other words the extermination of European Jewry.

The shift from persecution and expulsion to industrially organized genocide marked a dramatic escalation of policy, but not a change in the direction in which policy had been heading. The historiography of the Holocaust has been marked for many years by a dispute between 'intentionalists', who emphasize the role of conscious decisions by individuals, above all Hitler, in the genocide, and 'functionalists', who stress the role of accident, instrumental rationality, and bureaucratic decision making in bringing it about. This controversy has produced good points on both sides. The best option appears to me a combination of both views, but with an intentionalist bias.

Central to any explanation for the Holocaust should, on the intentionalist side, be the ideological motivation of the extreme racial antisemitism that Hitler and the Nazi leadership shared. They appear to have believed that they were at war with 'the Jews', who – as a race of parasitical sub-humans – were behind the communist threat as well as resistance by the Western democracies, and therefore had to be eradicated entirely to protect the Aryan race, especially the Teutonic Germans. They also had a Utopian vision, tinged with a perverted form of modern progressivism, that eliminating the Jews would eugenically allow for a racially healthy European populace, better suited to the technologically advanced society and economy of the 'New Order'. Given the hierarchical power structures by which the Nazis, with their *Führerprinzip*, operated, it needed only relatively few at the top, above all Hitler, to believe in this paranoid vision, and to be willing to act on it, for it to result in mass genocide.

Another vital enabling factor, however, was the more functionalist role of self-interested instrumental rationality, or opportunism. The Holocaust and antisemitism's success cannot be understood without a grasp of what Alexander Herzen once called 'rational evil'. Many might not have been convinced by the ideology, but *enough* were quite prepared to go along with the plan, because this offered them good jobs, rapid promotion, excellent business opportunities, the chance to acquire (Jewish) property cheaply, and, in the case of right-wing politicians in other countries, the chance to vanquish domestic rivals by riding German coat-tails. The cumulative effect of this was so powerful as to appear inexorable. For many individuals faced with an order linked to genocide, the choice was between compliance and death; and even if non-compliance only meant an end to one's career or livelihood, self-interest could overcome moral doubts by the argument that the order would be carried out in any case by the next man, so why suffer personally for no effect?

It is quite difficult to distinguish between the ideological and the practical motivation for participating in the Holocaust. A striking statistic about the Nazi genocide has been that produced by Simon Wiesenthal, who claimed that (former) Austrians in positions in the death machine were responsible for roughly half of the approximately six million Jews murdered between 1939 and 1945. This is extraordinary given that Austrians were only a tenth of the population of the Third Reich in 1939. Yet the figure becomes explicable when two factors are combined: first, the relative strength of antisemitism, also extreme racial antisemitism, in Vienna and Austria between the wars created a larger pool of those willing to contemplate such action; second, the fact that local Nazis were displaced by Germans from leading positions in the local hierarchy after 1938, and hence were forced to accept more marginal and less comfortable positions within the party structure: in order to succeed, they therefore opted for the undesirable but potentially career-enhancing postings in the concentration camps and associated institutions.

Similar ambivalence marks the question of how the Holocaust was allowed to occur, when a decade before it would have struck most Germans as unimaginable. A partial explanation, championed by Daniel Jonah Goldhagen, would be that the sophisticated propaganda efforts of the Nazis, led by Joseph Goebbels, had succeeded in indoctrinating the German populace in the idea of a Jewish world conspiracy, which threatened the very existence of the Teutonic race, and which, in a time of war, justified taking extreme measures, such as 'transporting' Jews to the East. Evidence suggesting most Germans knew, or strongly suspected, that this meant sending Jews to their deaths strengthens the case of successful indoctrination, and makes highly problematic postwar claims by Germans that 'we did not know'. On the other hand, the explanation from apathy, posited by Ian Kershaw and outlined above, also could explain such lack of resistance: indoctrination could well have failed, and yet any moral doubts about Nazi policy towards the Jews might simply not have been strong enough to counter the power, as described by Christopher Browning, of social conformism, deference to authority, and the instinct of self-preservation, brought on by fear of the consequences of resistance, when a war was on.

The Holocaust also benefited from the use of many modern elements: bureaucratic efficiency, rational organization, anonymity, economic incentivization, and the employment of various technological innovations. Zygmunt Bauman and others are quite right to stress the way in which the Nazis used modernity to effect their ends, and even used such modern concepts as public hygiene, uniformity, and utility to justify their actions. They clearly relied on the power of social conformism, and a transfer of loyalty to the national collective (a modern concept), to overcome traditional limits on human action, such as the prohibition against murdering unarmed civilians in cold blood. Moreover, the German, Nietzschean critique of modernity that had preceded the Nazi takeover had already put into question such quaint concepts as individual human rights, and the sanctity of human life, as outmoded relics of an age when a 'slave-religion' – Christianity, heir of Judaism – had perverted modern ethics. The murder of Jews in an industrial process thus could be seen as part of a breaking of false, traditional taboos in the pursuit of a higher form of Germanic modernity that dispensed with the superficial restrictions of mere Western civilization in search of what Thomas Mann had once called true 'culture'. The fact that Jews had come to represent in the ideology of the radical Right precisely this superficial, rationalistic, democratic, cosmopolitan civilization, and were seen as foreign to the national community, only aided this sense that their destruction was warranted by this new, National Socialist version of modernity.

The responses of other European countries to Nazi pressure to hand over their Jews for extermination puts this complex causal relationship between ideological conviction and pragmatic opportunism, traditional authority and modernity, into some perspective. Some societies, such as the Danes, on the border of the Nazi empire, were willing and able, as a nation, to rescue *their* Jewish citizens from the Nazis. Other states, even though under fascist or authoritarian regimes, also resisted surrendering *their* Jews to the Nazis. In the case of the Italian army, there was a secret agreement not to hand over any Jews to the Nazis, a policy of procrastinating non-compliance that succeeded until the Germans' takeover in 1943. In France, the Vichy government was quite prepared to hand over 'foreign' Jews, in other words émigrés, but resisted handing over Jewish French citizens. Franco's Spain also resisted collaborating with Hitler on this issue. In Hungary, the reactionary Horthy government resisted handing over any Hungarian Jews, and even when it was replaced by a fascist regime more in line with Nazi thinking, the Jews who were sent to the Nazi death camps were first of all the more traditionalist Jews of eastern Hungary and the countryside, and only then the Jews from Budapest, who had been the 19th-century allies of the Magyars. And even then, a very large number of Budapestian Jews survived the war, hidden by friends and sympathizers, who viewed these individuals as 'one of us' and not 'them'. In Poland, on the other hand, where the national intelligentsia was in any case destroyed by both Germans and Soviets, Jews had never been fully integrated into the *nation* and had always been regarded as separate, apart, and so the Polish populace saw little reason to identify with their fellow Jewish Polish citizens, let alone the masses of actually foreign Jews whom the Germans brought in to exploit and then murder.

None of this excuses those who committed this evil, enabled it, or did nothing to stop it; understanding the rational aspects of the choices made only makes the immorality of those choices clearer, especially in the light of those communities and those individuals who did stand up for the values of compassion and human decency.

The Holocaust, in this perspective, was the result of a particular German type of modernity, which had its echoes in other European countries, but which was also partially resisted by the regimes in those other countries, because they had different views on the relationship of Jews to their state or nation. These other states as well regarded Jews ambivalently, and were quite prepared to sacrifice the human rights of foreign Jews for the sake of better relations with the German overlord, but they viewed Jews whom they regarded as citizens of their state, or allies of their nation, differently – because they did not share that Nazi version of modernity, in which *all* Jews were enemies, not just the 'foreign' ones. Partly they did this, as reactionary authoritarian regimes, out of regard to traditional values, but also because their version of modernity did not embrace this drastic rejection of what might be termed the 'pathos of humanity', but preserved it, often within a Christian form.

If this was so for the countries allied with Nazi Germany, it was much more the case with the Western Allies. The policies of the Western Allies have been rightly criticized for not doing enough to rescue more Jews and for not doing enough to stop the death machine by, for instance, bombing rail lines to Auschwitz. It is further the case that the potential for mass discrimination, mass imprisonment and persecution, and unjustified mass killing of civilians is also latent within the American and British versions of modernity, as episodes during the Second World War with Japanese Americans and many subsequent episodes such as My Lai attest. Yet the version of modernity that resulted in the Holocaust came out of a culture and a society in which a version of modernity that offered an *alternative* to Western liberal democratic, capitalist modernity had long been championed, and in which antisemitism, an ideological perversion that requires holistic, collectivist, and corporatist thought to be cogent, could flourish. It is that holistic, German Central European modernity, and not the liberal modernity of the West, that gave rise to the Holocaust.

13. Auschwitz: toothbrushes

Chapter 8
After Auschwitz

More than 60 years have passed since the cataclysmic consequence of antisemitism in the Holocaust. The time span between the beginnings of political antisemitism around 1880 and the Wannsee Conference of 1942 is now almost exactly the same as that between the Holocaust's end in 1945 and today. Over this long period, the relative strength and significance of antisemitism, and its place in the world, have radically changed. In the pre-Holocaust world, antisemitism might have been rejected by most in the liberal West as an irrational ideology, but in much of Europe it had informed government policy, and it appeared to be supported both by the modern, rational drive to create functioning national societies based on ethnicity, and on 'scientific' racial theories that were seen as harnessing the achievements of medical and biological science for the betterment and health of the human race, an attitude summed up in the phrase 'racial hygiene'. In the post-Holocaust world, antisemitism has come to be completely discredited, a 'chimeric' system of beliefs based on paranoia and illusion, and its 'scientific' support in racial theory has similarly been exposed as a fraud. Yet this transformation took time, and is not yet complete.

The change in attitudes did not happen overnight. Retrospectively, we might think that the horror of the Holocaust caused such revulsion at the consequences of the prejudice and racism that had brought it about, that it completely bankrupted the cause of antisemitism, ushering in an era of pluralism and tolerance that is still with us. Yet the historical record tells another story. In the immediate aftermath of the war, the major theme was confusion, and even when the concentration camps and death camps were captured and the scenes of horror broadcast to the world, the extent of the mass murder was not immediately evident, or for many even comprehensible, nor was it to be clear for quite some time that this was primarily a *Jewish* disaster, with its roots in antisemitism, rather than a general human tragedy based on man's inhumanity to man. The Holocaust was in actuality *both*, but for a long time the overwhelming part of it comprised by the attempted Nazi eradication of European Jewry was downplayed in many circles in favour of its more universalist aspect.

In some respects, the war's aftermath initially saw little change in previous attitudes. In Poland, Jewish survivors and returning refugees were often given a hostile reception by non-Jewish Poles concerned at Jews being given 'favoured treatment' by the Soviet 'liberators', and there was a series of pogroms, the most infamous being that in Kielce in 1946. In Britain, there was also a level of anti-Jewish sentiment that is difficult to imagine in hindsight. The problems being caused for Britain by the Jews in Palestine led to hostility towards Jews from many in the officialdom, and on a popular level there were also anti-Jewish riots in several British towns in the autumn of 1947. The Foreign Secretary, Ernest Bevin, displayed the uncomprehending mixture of national particularism and liberal universalism common in Britain at the time. He thought it preferable that surviving Polish Jews be reintegrated at 'home' in Poland rather than be allowed to immigrate to Britain. In his opinion, they would not be good material for assimilation to the norm of British society, which was his 'liberal universalist' goal for foreigners and minorities. Whereas many Holocaust survivors were allowed to immigrate to the United States, very few settled in Britain.

The major powers which responded most positively to the Jewish predicament after the Holocaust were the United States and the Soviet Union. American pluralist politics meant that, even though there was also a large degree of xenophobic and antisemitic sentiment in many quarters in American society, there was also a very influential body of support for policies to help Holocaust survivors and to respond to the Holocaust as a *Jewish* disaster. The policies of the Soviet Union were also, from 1945 to 1948, before the Cold War truly set in, relatively responsive to Jewish concerns, especially as regards Jewish attempts to establish a Jewish state in Palestine, which it saw as a future bulwark against Western imperialism. It was largely from this combination of American and Soviet policies and interests that 1948 saw three major international achievements that were, at least in part, answers to the Holocaust and the Jewish crisis it had so hideously underlined: the Convention on the Prevention and Punishment of the Crime of Genocide; the Universal Declaration of Human Rights; and the recognition of the newly established state of Israel (with Soviet *de jure* recognition long before American, and admission to the United Nations on 11 May 1949).

These agreements, in the long term, set the stage for a radical change in the relationship between Jews and antisemitism, yet it still took many decades for that change to develop. Indeed, the comity of superpower interests that enabled the 1948 agreements soon dissolved in the onset of the Cold War. In the Soviet Bloc, the relatively pro-Jewish stance taken until then experienced drastic transformation into its virtual opposite: an anti-Zionism that served as a thin disguise for renewed antisemitism based on a form of ideologically transmuted nationalism. Partly this was due to Stalin's disappointment that socialist-dominated Israel did not take the Soviet side in the Cold War but remained neutral; partly as well, it arose from alarm at the re-emergence of a strong sense of Jewish identity among Soviet Jews, as a reaction to the Holocaust and as a response to the triumphant establishment of the state of Israel. Then again, it is also partly explained by the self-interest of communist apparatchiks in the Soviet Union and its various satellites. They could use the Jewish origins of many of their better-positioned comrades to exploit nationalist xenophobic and antisemitic prejudice to accuse these 'bourgeois cosmopolitans' and 'Zionist agents' of treason, leading to their removal by execution, and the freeing up of plum positions in the communist apparatus for the supposedly more loyal and patriotic, non-Jewish party members. In the case of the show trial in 1951–2 of Rudolf Slánský and his supposed co-conspirators, ten out of thirteen being of Jewish origin, Klement Gottwald could also prove his loyalty to Stalin by sacrificing Slánský. The 'discovery' of the Doctors' Plot in January 1953 in the Soviet Union, supposedly hatched by 'corrupt Jewish bourgeois nationalists', almost led to major persecution of Jews, only precluded by Stalin's death.

The post-Stalin years saw better conditions for Jews in the Soviet Bloc and improved relations with Israel, but after the events of 1967 the Soviet Union increasingly followed an anti-Zionist line abroad and an anti-Jewish policy at home, persecuting and discriminating against those Jewish citizens who insisted on retaining their Jewish identity and religion, and hence their difference. Then again, it was virtually impossible for Soviet Jews to cease being 'Jewish'. What had originally appeared as a progressive measure of revolutionary Bolshevism after 1917, the recognition of (equal) nationalities under the Soviet umbrella, had included Jews as one of the nationalities. This meant that, believing or not, committed to a Jewish identity or not, an individual of Jewish 'nationality' was a Jew as far as the Soviet state was concerned, and could do nothing to change it, or escape the discrimination that came with this status.

In the non-communist West as well, the general mindset that had tolerated and often encouraged antisemitic attitudes, and also policies, was not so easily shifted. The Second World War was not, for the most part, seen as a triumph of universal human rights over racism, let alone antisemitism, but rather in nationalist terms, as the victory of the Allied nations against the Axis Powers, primarily the Germans and Japanese. Each country saw the war in its own terms, of humiliating defeat in many cases, heroic national resistance in some, and liberation in most. The British saw the war as their 'finest hour' in which they had 'stood alone' against Nazi tyranny, and 1945 was viewed as a national vindication. The other European 'victors', especially the Soviet Union, also saw the war in this nationalist perspective. The idea that the greatest war crime committed in the war had been against an international ethnic group, the Jews, did not fit into this schema. Even when the war was seen in ideological terms, it was either seen as the triumph of 'freedom' against Nazi totalitarianism, or of 'socialism' against capitalistic fascism, and, again, the particularist, ethnic dimension of the Jewish disaster was secondary to this at best.

Part of the reason for the initial Western inability fully to recognize the racist aspect to the Holocaust was that racial thinking was still an integral and accepted part of the Western political universe. The US Army that had contributed so centrally to defeating Nazism was itself still segregated along racial lines in 1945, and it was only in 1948 that Harry S. Truman, against stiff resistance, ordered desegregation in the American armed forces. Britain, France, and other European powers such as the Netherlands and Portugal still held in 1945 extensive overseas empires whose underlying justification was the supposed superiority of the white race over the 'lesser' races, and the right and duty ('white man's burden') that followed to civilize the natives – the 'mission civilisatrice'. Although the American administrations of Roosevelt and Truman both contributed greatly to speeding the dissolution of these colonial empires, other branches of American thinking were shot through with racist assumptions about white, 'Aryan' superiority – at home and abroad. This racial thinking did not always work to the detriment of Jews; in an ironic repetition of the dynamic of 'negative integration', in South Africa and the United States Jews 'made the cut' as 'whites', hence they probably benefited as being members of 'us' rather than 'them'.

Nevertheless, the persistence of this racial mindset still allowed antisemitic theories to appear rational, and the idea of determining policy by biology legitimate, to the long-term endangerment of the Jews' position within Western society.

The onset of the Cold War also had negative consequences for Jews in the West. McCarthyism in America led to a resurgence of the charge against Jews of political radicalism, which was a skewed reflection of the reality that American Jews were generally to be found on the political Left, and that many Jewish individuals, especially many émigrés, were prominent in the liberal and left-wing intelligentsia. The Cold War also diverted the attention of the Western powers from the prosecution of Nazi war criminals, and hence relieved pressure on such countries as Austria, where antisemitism had been especially strong, and remained so well into the 1950s, from dealing fully with their citizens' responsibility for the Holocaust. As a counterpart, the creation of East Germany led to a situation where only one western 'half' of Germany acknowledged responsibility for the genocide committed against the Jews, while the communist 'half' cast itself in the role of the heir to the fighters *against* fascism, and hence as a victim not a perpetrator.

Yet West Germany, under the leadership of Konrad Adenauer, did accept responsibility for what the Nazi state had perpetrated, and set out to compensate Nazism's Jewish victims accordingly. It also, under the guidance of the Western occupation forces, especially the Americans, instituted programmes to re-educate the German populace about antisemitism and its horrific consequences. Germans therefore had a head start on the major change in attitudes towards Jews and antisemitism that occurred after 1948.

In Germany, this was largely due to direct re-education, but in other countries the improvement of the Jewish position within Western society was as much caused by more general factors that had only an indirect relation to the 'lessons' of the Holocaust.

One such factor was the collapse of European imperialism in the postwar era, which burst the balloon of theories of white, and hence 'Aryan', supremacy. An even more significant factor must be the discrediting of racial thinking generally. Although at first sight there appears to be no direct link to Jews and antisemitism, the struggle for civil rights by African-Americans in the postwar era, into the 1960s, gave a strong impulse to changing American society's approach to racial and ethnic divisions generally, and both fed into and benefited from the development of the pluralist model that came to dominate not only the American political scene, but also that of Western Europe. It is no coincidence that many of the most prominent 'white' figures in the American civil rights movement were Jewish, nor was it mere coincidence that many of the most prominent intellectual progenitors and champions of the prevailing ideology of liberal pluralism were also Jewish, many of them émigrés, for there was an obvious community of interest for blacks and Jews to discredit racism and antisemitism. By so doing, they mutually provided themselves an accepted place within the American political universe. Tearing down barriers for one also meant tearing down barriers for the other.

Liberalization and openness to a more pluralist approach also worked against antisemitism, and for Jewish interests, in the world of religion. The Second Vatican Council of 1962–5 was primarily about modernization of the Catholic Church, but it also produced a major re-evaluation of Christian-Jewish relations, chapter four of the conciliar declaration *Nostra aetate*. Crucially, as it were, this chapter relieved Jewry of the traditional Christian accusation of being 'Christ killers', and sought to see the Jewish religion positively, rejecting old Catholic theology about the New Covenant displacing the Old, and instead seeing the covenant between God and the Jews as still valid, and the Jewish tradition a vital element of Christianity. This, and subsequent, close negotiation and discussion between the Catholic Church hierarchy and Jewish leaders, as well as with other Christian denominations, has produced a revolutionary change in

Christian-Jewish relations, at least on a theological and denominational level.

The political and economic recasting of Western Europe after 1945 also, eventually, had a profound impact on the place of Jews in society, and has resulted in the almost complete marginalization of antisemitism. The process of Europeanization that has resulted in today's European Union began with the explicit mission to make Europe's nation states, particularly France and Germany, so inter-dependent economically that nationalist wars, such as had plagued the continent for a century or more, would no longer be possible. This process both ushered in a period of remarkable economic growth and complicated European national identities and loyalties in a way that has redounded very much to the favour of European Jews, and made antisemitism an insignificant, discredited force in European political and social life.

Prosperity has made the politics of envy that lay behind much of the popularity of antisemitism in the late 19th century and again in the interwar years largely redundant, much as it has also undercut the vehemence behind the class conflicts between 'capitalist' and 'worker'. The diversification of loyalty and identity that has resulted from the opening up of the nation state's monopoly both at the top – with multilateralist decision making on a European level – and at the bottom – with decentralization and devolution of power to localities, regions, and autonomous provinces – has also encouraged a more open, inclusive approach to minorities and 'others' generally, Jews very much included. The situation in Europe regarding Jews and antisemitism is far from being perfect, especially in the former 'Eastern European' countries freed from Soviet hegemony in 1989, and the point should be made that one reason for the relative acceptance of Jews in Europe today is that there are so few of them, due to the Holocaust. Yet it is also true that the Jewish situation in Europe represents a vast improvement, generally speaking, on the situation in the 1950s, let alone that of the 1930s. The success of pluralism, and in recent years of postmodern multicultural approaches, means that Jews in Europe, as in North America, can increasingly claim a definite, 'different' Jewish identity and yet still be viewed as full members of whichever political community they live in. Even in historically 'liberal' countries such as the United States, Britain, and France, such an assertion of Jewish identity within the national community would have been far less socially acceptable, or approved, or even possible, 50 years ago. The postmodern, pluralist notion of 'diversity within unity' that dominates Western political thinking has been an especial boon for Diaspora Jewry.

Antisemitism, as antisemitism, has, in contrast, been completely discredited in respectable Western public opinion. Partly this is due to the radical change in attitudes towards racism and ethno-nationalism generally, but the memory of the Holocaust has, over the long term, come to be a very effective inhibitor of antisemitic demagoguery. Since the 1970s, the Jewish dimension of the Holocaust was made more evident to the Western public in a wave of films and television programmes, and remembrance of the Holocaust became not only a German and Israeli phenomenon, but also a part of American culture, as embodied in the Holocaust Museum (funded 1980, opened 1993). This memorialization and integration into national memory has spread around the (Western) world. The Holocaust and the horrific consequences of antisemitism are, ironically, more central to Western consciousness today than they were in 1960, or even 1945. In this way, accusing 'the Jews' has come to be immediately associated in the public's mind with images of mass murder and human depravity, so as to make such attacks far more dangerous to the accuser than the accused.

One sign of the effectiveness of the Holocaust as an obstacle to antisemitism is that one of the main forms of 'antisemitic' expression still available in the public sphere, but strongly contested by Jewish defence organizations such as the

Anti-Defamation League, is Holocaust-denial. The idea that antisemitism, if left unchecked, leads to the horrors of genocide as evidenced in the Holocaust has become so established in Western opinion that only by denying that the Holocaust ever took place can antisemites even begin to lay out their accusations against Jews. This is second- or even third-stage antisemitism, for it refers to claims about past actions against Jews, rather than making any direct accusations against current Jews (except in as much as there is the suspicion among many deniers that Jews have invented the historical record to subjugate guilty non-Jews to their will). Even this rather remote form of antisemitism has been set very much on the defensive, and in David Irving's case, routed in court, as the historical evidence of the crimes of the Nazis and their collaborators against the Jews has been proved beyond a reasonable doubt.

Politicians on the radical Right, such as Jean-Marie le Pen, who has minimized the importance of the Holocaust, and Jörg Haider, who has talked of members of the Waffen-SS as 'decent people', have more recently been at pains to assure the public that they are not antisemitic. This is probably because even on the far right end of the political spectrum, it has become clear that antisemitic posturing brings little or no political gain, and is more trouble than it is worth. In any case, talking up the threat of Muslim immigrants is far more effective, and just as easy to integrate into nationalist, radical right-wing ideology. Right-wing politicians can even pretend to be supporters and defenders of Europe's Jewish communities against attacks by Islamist terrorists and their alleged supporters among Islamic immigrants and asylum seekers.

Eastern Europe, or rather the parts of Central and Eastern Europe formerly on the other side of the Iron Curtain, has since the liberation of 1989 seen a re-emergence of forms of political antisemitism that hearken back to the interwar era, promoting a poisonous mix of integral nationalism laced with conservative authoritarianism and religious bigotry. The probability that such attitudes – amounting to an antisemitism without Jews in much of the region (if not in Hungary) – might emerge from the political deep freeze of the communist era was already made starkly clear by Claude Lanzmann's epic film *Shoah* from 1985, and indeed they have. The initial success of democratization and liberalization in the former Soviet Bloc countries raised hopes that such views would fade away with more prosperous times and the process of joining the European Union, and for a long while they did appear to wane. In Poland, in particular, there was substantial progress in facing up to the horrors of the past, and even the development of a slightly strange *philo*semitism, seen for instance in the revival of *klezmer* music. Pope John Paul II, for all his doctrinal conservatism, did much to improve Catholic-Jewish relations, and some of this was felt back in his homeland.

Hopes for such a positive transformation have recently received setbacks, given events in Poland and Hungary especially. The readiness of apparently respectable politicians to play the card of xenophobia and lightly disguised Jew-hatred is deeply unfortunate. Yet these developments need to be kept in perspective: blatant political antisemitism remains a fringe phenomenon, and the anti-Jewish attitudes on display are largely a recrudescence of interwar attitudes, modified by experiences of the communist era. There are strong trends going the other way as well. The membership of many of these countries in the European Union sets distinct limits, formal and informal, to such reactionary politics, and the ongoing 'Europeanization' of the region will, in all likelihood, quiet these old ghosts.

New forms of antisemitism have emerged since 1945, but they differ in major respects from the forms of antisemitism that led to the Holocaust. One particularly tragic form of antisemitism has been the African-American antisemitism that emerged in the wake of the civil rights movement. Having made impressive, mutually beneficial gains in achieving racial equality and a more inclusive, pluralistic understanding of American identity, the

Jewish–African-American alliance splintered on the rocks of ethnic division, as African-American radical groups, such as Malcolm X's Nation of Islam and Black Nationalists, identified Jews with the oppressive white majority, and as many Jews, especially in the nascent neo-conservative movement, decided that accommodating black demands for affirmative action and other 'privileges' was antithetical to the conservative small government, market-based liberalism that they now espoused. Jewish racial fear of 'ghetto blacks' also led to Jews joining the 'white flight' from the inner cities, exacerbating black economic and social resentment that Jews had betrayed them and the cause for racial equality. What has resulted has been an at times threatening combination of economic and ethnic hostility against Jews, similar to that of the minority nationalities in the Habsburg Monarchy. There the Jews were seen as allies of the dominant, oppressing 'state-peoples', just as American Jews, in Hollywood for instance, are seen as part of the white, excluding establishment, rather than as allies in the fight for equality. On the other hand, while the rhetoric of black leaders such as Louis Farrakhan has been at times distasteful and worse, and while more respectable leaders such as Jesse Jackson and Andrew Young have also made statements suggesting underlying anti-Jewish resentments, there remains a large comity of interests and also values between the Jewish and African-American communities and their leaderships, especially in the political realm.

One of the stranger forms of antisemitism that has emerged in recent years has been that in East Asia, most notably in Japan, where there are very few Jews. On closer inspection, however, this antisemitism without Jews shows just how far the status of Jews and thus antisemitism has changed. The main thrust of Japanese claims against Jews reflects the influence of antisemitic accusations of Jewish world conspiracy, much on the lines of the *Protocols of the Elders of Zion*, that 'the Jews' are a strong economic force in the world that needs to be countered. What is somewhat different about much of this Japanese approach, however, is that there is more than a touch of admiration of Jews in this attitude, in that Japanese marvel at how such a small group could have such a large amount of power and influence over world affairs. Japanese 'antisemitic' commentators do not so much want to destroy the Jewish 'conspiracy' as emulate the Jews' supposed techniques and strategies of control.

While the Japanese are not 'from Mars', it is worth stepping back and looking through their eyes at the Jewish position in Western society, at the role that Jewish individuals play in the financial, commercial, political, entertainment, intellectual, cultural, scientific, and media world today, to see how cogent such a 'conspiratorial' view can be. For it remains a truly remarkable phenomenon as to just how successful and influential individual Jews, and individuals of Jewish descent, are in today's world, despite being members of a tiny ethnic minority, of around 0.2% of the world's population (roughly 13,000,000 in a world population of over 6,400,000,000). Even in the United States, with a Jewish population of over 5 million, Jews account for less than 2% of the total population. No matter how you look at it, the role of Jews in Western society is completely disproportionate to their numbers, and almost invites ideas of conspiracy by members of other less successful ethnic groups. Given the human inclination to explain one's own problems by the unfair advantages taken by others, what is remarkable about Jews and antisemitism in the world today is not how much antisemitic sentiment and prejudice remains in Western societies, but how little.

The one area where anti-Jewish hostility has apparently continued to flourish and be respectable, to the disgust and trepidation of many Jews, has been in attitudes to Zionism, Israel, and the Israeli/Palestinian conflict. This too is a post-Auschwitz phenomenon. Zionism, and its claim to Jewish national rights to a *Judenstaat* (properly translated as a 'state for the Jews' but usually translated as a 'Jewish state'), had been working to change the Jewish position in the world and Jewish identity since the late

19th century, and had already made a major impact in recasting Jewish and non-Jewish understandings of Jewishness before the Holocaust. Yet it was the establishment of the state of Israel in 1948 that really began the major change in how Jewish affairs are seen, by Jews and non-Jews (and antisemites) alike, today. Today attitudes towards Israel are seen by many as a more accurate gauge of 'antisemitic' or 'philosemitic' sentiment than attitudes or behaviour towards Jews in one's own society. The claim has been made by many commentators that there is a 'new antisemitism' that, instead of attacking Jews on an economic, political, cultural, or racial basis within the various national societies, now has transferred its hostility to the plane of international society, so that the enemy has become one big 'Jew', the state of Israel, and its Zionist supporters. Anti-Zionism, it is claimed, is the new antisemitism.

There is an undoubted overlap between hostility to the Zionist movement and the state of Israel, and the tradition of antisemitism outlined in the pages above. To equate anti-Zionism and antisemitism is, however, far too simplistic, theoretically crass, and demeans the memory of those who suffered the horrendous consequences of real antisemitism. It is true that, since Zionism's founding and the establishment of a large and ever-growing Jewish community in Palestine, there has also been a burgeoning of an Arab and Muslim antisemitism that had not previously existed. It is further true that Arab nationalists from the 1930s onwards adopted Nazi antisemitic tropes to bolster their case against the Jewish settlement in Palestine; and that the Arab and Soviet opposition to Israel after 1948, and especially after Israel's victory in 1967, a hostility that led to the passing of the UN resolution in 1975 citing Zionism as 'a form of racism and racial discrimination', was informed by various antisemitic ideas, such as that of the Jewish world conspiracy popularized by the *Protocols of the Elders of Zion*. The adaptation of this notorious forgery into a serialization on Arab television is ample evidence of the ways in which antisemitic tropes have been introduced into the Arab and

14. *The Jewish Danger: The Protocols of the Elders of Zion*, French edition (c. 1940). First published in Russian in 1903, the forged account of an alleged Jewish world conspiracy has appeared in many languages, including Arabic, and recently appeared as a dramatic serialization on Arabian television.

Muslim world, and severely affected the image of Jews in that world, and in much of the developing world as well. Moreover, this hostility to Zionism and the Jewish state has been transferred to Jews generally, as part of the supposedly conspiratorial 'Jewish nation', and has come back to Europe and North America in the form of hostility by many Muslims and their supporters to Jews. In the United States, this has sometimes taken the form of African-American hostility to Jews as the counterpart to support for the Palestinian cause, as in the case of the Nation of Islam; in Europe, many if not most attacks against Jewish targets in such countries as France are no longer perpetrated by disaffected, right-wing radical, native youths, but by young North African immigrants or 'first-generation' French Muslims.

This is all fairly obviously true, and the resurgence of attacks on Jews in Europe that it has occasioned very distressing, but it is also fairly obviously due not to antisemitism as such, but rather Arab and Muslim resistance, revenge, and general hostility to the Zionist achievement of a Jewish state in Israel. It cannot be said, as it has so often about racial antisemitism in Europe, that Arab 'antisemitism' has no rational cause. Had Israel not existed as a Jewish nation state, it is difficult to see why this Arab and Muslim antisemitism would have emerged the way it has. The irony is that the movement of political Zionism that Theodor Herzl created had as its leading principle the idea that the creation of the Jews' own nation state, and the removal of most of European Jewry to that state, would 'solve' the problem of antisemitism by removing its main cause. If anti-Zionism has now given birth to an even more threatening form of 'new antisemitism', then this suggests that the whole theoretical basis of Zionism, at least as Herzl understood it, was mistaken, and Zionism as an ideology bankrupt. Fortunately for Zionists, for the future of the state of Israel, and for all opponents of antisemitism and other forms of racial and ethnic prejudice, the equation between anti-Zionism and antisemitism is deeply flawed.

After Auschwitz

Anti-Zionism is not necessarily equatable with antisemitism. Antisemites can oppose the idea of the Jewish 'nation' having its own state, as they oppose Jews having any power or freedom. Yet it is also the case that many moderate or even radical 'antisemites' before 1945 supported Zionism's recognition of the Jews as a separate nation, and also encouraged Jewish migration to Palestine, which they saw as, following Herzl's argument, relieving the European nations of the 'Jewish Problem'. Obversely, many opponents of antisemitic discrimination, holding true to the liberal ideology of emancipation, and seeing Jews as a primarily religious group, rejected Zionism as a false analysis of the Jewish Question, forcing Jewish individuals into a *national* Jewish identification that they did not have, and that compromised their membership in the various European nation states or nationalities.

Many principled defenders of the rights of Jews on the political Left, whether liberal or socialist, did so on the basis of Jews' rights as full, equal citizens of the civic nation or of a universal humanity, and therefore rejected Zionism as creating an unnecessary and false barrier to Jewish integration. Many Jewish leaders before the Holocaust also criticized Zionism on these grounds, and also on religious grounds, from both reformed and traditionalist perspectives. The left-wing anti-Zionism so prevalent in Western Europe today is partly based on the same rejection of the idea of Jewish *national* identity, and this does not necessarily at all impinge on the defence by the same left-wing figures of the rights of individual Jews, or even Jewish communities, within the domestic polity. In such cases, anti-Zionism cannot in any proper sense be equated with antisemitism. Moreover, this left-wing perspective compounds its anti-Zionism by reiterating the support for equal rights it shows domestically for Jews by transposing this same support onto equal rights for Palestinians within the context of the Middle East conflict.

The degree to which European public opinion is 'anti-Zionist' has, in any case, been distorted and exaggerated in the American media. Most Europeans, also those on the Left, accept and support Israel's existence as a state. What they object to is what they see as unnecessarily harsh policies of Israeli governments against the Palestinian populace. There is also a clear disquiet about the infringement of principles of fairness with regard to how much Israel and its Western supporters, primarily in the United States, are prepared to give to the Palestinians in any long-term settlement of the conflict. If there is more emphasis put on Israeli responsibility to reach a just solution, and more emphasis put on this ethnic conflict over territory and resources than on the many others in the world, then this is not due so much to antisemitism as to, ironically, European acceptance of Israel, the Jewish state, as a civilized and hence more responsible member of the international community, and the centrality, also today, of Jews within the Western Judaeo-Christian tradition and world view.

There is also a deeper irony in some of the contemporary European criticism of Israel, from an anti-nationalistic standpoint. Herzlian Zionism thought that the way to prevent antisemitism was to accept the 'either/or' logic of nationalism by setting up a separate ethno-national state for Jews outside of Europe, thus removing conflict by removing difference. Yet the ultimate lesson learned by Western Europeans (and indeed by Americans) about antisemitism's causes and its consequence in genocide was that monolithic, conformist nationalism, apparently the most advanced form of modernity in mid-20th-century Europe, was the root cause of this political and moral human disaster. Continental Europeans responded to this by setting in train the process that has led to a dissolving of the boundaries and prerogatives of the nation state, and allowing, potentially, a far more open and inclusive approach to self-definition and self-identification by Europeans, in which Jews – and Muslims – should be able to be full participants, as themselves rather than having to assimilate to some prescribed, overly uniform norm.

In such countries as Britain and the United States, in which more liberal and pluralistic traditions persisted from another (perhaps more old-fashioned) form of modernity, the *modus vivendi* of the 'heterogeneous nation state' and 'political pluralism' had stood up much more effectively (though not perfectly) to the same temptations of mass discrimination, persecution, and extermination. They were the systems that won, and preserved human dignity and freedom. Yet even they, over the succeeding years, have seen the injustices and dangers in the remaining elements of repressive conformity and uniformity within them, whether of a racist or 'liberal universalist' nature. Many commentators, especially on the progressive Left, have also recognized the dangers inherent in even the 'liberal' nationalism that these states represent, let alone their ethno-nationalist alternatives. It is therefore nationalism, with its 'for us or against us' exclusion of difference, that is seen as the greatest threat, historically as well as presently, to that acceptance of other interests, other points of view, and 'others', that provides the basis of pluralist liberal democracy. Hence nationalism is seen as the most potent source of the prejudice, intolerance, and hatred of 'the other' that is the basis of antisemitism and other racial and group hatreds.

This rejection of nationalism as the dominant form of modern social and political organization does not leave any clear successors. The sometimes heated argument between 'liberal pluralists' and 'multiculturalists' over who is the more authentic heir to emancipation's mantle is a sign of this. The degree to which the individual or his/her group should be seen as the source of value and meaning is a postmodern argument that is far from over. It can be seen also in continuing debate about the spiritual heritage of Jews to the West, and their place in that world. Hence on one side of the postmodern debate Jewish figures such as Jacques Derrida are seen as having opened a space for 'difference' within Western philosophy precisely out of the Jewish experience of the consequences of insisting on a lack of difference. On the other, postmodernists such as Jan Assmann point to the fact, often commented on by anti-Jewish thinkers going back to Antiquity, that the monotheism that Egyptians created and Jews adopted and proliferated is antithetical to the multicultural embrace of pantheistic difference of the postmodern world of diversity. Such debates show that the ancient dialectic that has governed Jewish history, between particularism and universalism, inclusion and exclusion, both on the Jewish and non-Jewish side, will ever continue.

Yet the idea that the nation state should be absolutely sovereign over individual and group interests is an idea that, despite what right-wing American ideologues might believe, is rapidly losing cogency in our diversified and globalized world. Moreover, in a world determined ever more by relations, by connections and links, rather than by territorial control and borders, relying on ethno-national states makes ever less sense, politically or morally. This is very beneficial to the Jewish Diaspora, indeed it is a sort of ideal situation, whereby Jews can be Jews in their religious and ethnic community, around the world, and still be embraced as full citizens and members of their respective political and cultural, 'national' communities, whether as Americans, Germans, or even Europeans. Yet such developments are not so easy for the 'Jewish state' of Israel to embrace, for it was founded as a classic ethno-national state, and, with all its forms of liberal democracy, remains so at base. This is not to say that it should not continue in this form, or that this is unacceptable as such; but what it does show is that European disquiet over Israel and what it stands for does make some sense from the postmodern European perspective.

If there is a conclusion to be drawn about the history of antisemitism as it applies to the situation of Jews around the world today, and particularly to the Israeli/Palestinian conflict, it is that difference should not be denied, obliterated, or persecuted, but should be accepted, respected, and an honest and diligent attempt made to understand it. Antisemites in the late 19th century and after were intent on not allowing Jewish difference, and on seeing that difference as an undivided and threatening, destructive mass. They refused to recognize that Jewish views should be respected and had their own validity; they denied that Jews differed among themselves, and saw a 'Jewish mind' that all Jews supposedly shared and a 'Jewish conspiracy' that all Jews were in on, so that capitalism and socialism were just part of the same phenomenon. Antisemites were also incapable of differentiating in their own minds between a particular ethnic group, the Jews, and the much larger historical events of modernization and modernity with which Jews were indeed associated, but for which they alone were far from wholly responsible. This refusal to accept difference led to moral disaster.

In return, in viewing current debates about antisemitism, especially 'new antisemitism', it seems pertinent to point out that not all antisemites, those harbouring or expressing some hostility to Jews in some form or another, are the same or suffering from the same psychic or moral disorders. Some critics of Jews today view them as persisting in a particularistic tradition that prevents a truly universal humanity, while others see the Jewish tradition as imposing a deadening, uniform universalism that denies pantheistic, multicultural diversity; some see, as they ever did, Jews as a threat to their own cultural and social superiority, while others see those same Jews as the allies of the oppressive ruling race or class. All of these sources can lead to anti-Jewish resentment and anti-Jewish behaviour, and some of them have irrational sources, but others have sources that, at some level, are quite rational. For those who wish to ensure that Jews never again are faced with the disaster of the Holocaust, the best strategy against such multifarious hostilities would appear to be not to opt for one, particular solution that applies exclusively to Jews. Rather, the best way to navigate these shoals of enmity is to engage the support of all other forms of difference, and, united against false unities, build a society, and a global community, in which a small minority such as the Jews will be protected by a consensus that ensuring and respecting the rights and interests of the few are also in the interests and tradition of the many.

Antisemitism, in the form of a political movement aimed at persecuting, discriminating against, removing, or even exterminating Jews is no longer a major threat in our globalized world. Yet antisemitism in the form of resentment at Jewish success and Jewish power, whether illusory or not, and in the form of social and cultural dislike or prejudice, will persist as long as there are Jews, just as would be the case for any other identifiable ethnic or religious group. The question is how can this 'eternal' form of antisemitism be kept within minimal and 'harmless' dimensions. In those terms, the answer to antisemitism is ultimately not a Jewish state, but the establishment of a truly global system of liberal pluralism.

References and further reading

Author's note: The following books are sorted only roughly according to relevance to the specific chapters. Many, if not most, touch on subjects in several chapters.

1. What is antisemitism?

Hannah Arendt, *Antisemitism* (San Diego: Harvest/HBJ, 1985)

Sander L. Gilman, *Jewish Self-Hatred: Anti-Semitism and the Hidden Language of the Jews* (Baltimore: The Johns Hopkins University Press, 1986)

Sander L. Gilman and Steven T. Katz (eds), *Anti-Semitism in Times of Crisis* (New York: New York University Press, 1991)

Jacob Katz, *From Prejudice to Destruction: Anti-Semitism, 1700–1933* (Cambridge, MA: Harvard University Press, 1980)

Gavin I. Langmuir, *Toward a Definition of Antisemitism* (Berkeley and Los Angeles: University of California Press, 1990)

Richard S. Levy (ed.), *Antisemitism: A Historical Encyclopedia of Prejudice and Persecution*, 2 vols (Santa Barbara: ABC Clio, 2005)

Albert S. Lindemann, *Esau's Tears: Modern Anti-Semitism and the Rise of the Jews* (Cambridge: Cambridge University Press, 1997)

Peter Pulzer, *The Rise of Political Anti-Semitism in Germany and Austria*, revised edn. (London: Peter Halban, 1988)

Jehuda Reinharz and Paul Mendes-Flohr (eds), *The Jew in the Modern World* (Oxford: Oxford University Press, 1980)

Jean-Paul Sartre, *Anti-Semite and Jew* (New York: Schocken, 1948)

Robert S. Wistrich, *Antisemitism: The Longest Hatred* (New York: Pantheon, 1991)

2. The burden of the past

David Biale, *Power and Powerlessness in Jewish History* (New York: Schocken, 1986)

Daniel Chirot and Anthony Reid (eds), *Essential Outsiders: Chinese and Jews in the Modern Transformation of Southeast Asia and Central Europe* (Seattle: University of Washington Press, 1997)

Gary B. Cohen, *The Politics of Ethnic Survival: Germans in Prague, 1861–1914* (Princeton: Princeton University Press, 1981)

David Feldman, *Englishmen and Jews: Social Relations and Political Culture, 1840–1914* (New Haven: Yale University Press, 1994)

Gavin I. Langmuir, *History, Religion and Antisemitism* (Berkeley and Los Angeles: University of California Press, 1990)

Albert S. Lindemann, *Anti-Semitism before the Holocaust* (Harlow: Longman, 2000)

William O. McCagg Jr, *A History of Habsburg Jews, 1670–1918* (Bloomington: Indiana University Press, 1989)

Michael A. Meyer (ed.), *German-Jewish History in Modern Times*, vol. 1 (New York: Columbia University Press, 1996)

3. The Chosen People

Steven Beller, *Vienna and the Jews, 1867–1938: A Cultural History* (Cambridge: Cambridge University Press, 1989)

Jonathan Frankel, *Prophecy and Politics: Socialism, Nationalism and the Russian Jews, 1862–1917* (Cambridge: Cambridge University Press, 1981)

Arthur Hertzberg, *The French Enlightenment and the Jews* (New York: Columbia University Press, 1968)

Jacob Katz, *Out of the Ghetto: The Social Background of Jewish Emancipation, 1770–1870* (Cambridge, MA: Harvard University Press, 1973)

John Doyle Klier, *Imperial Russia's Jewish Question, 1855–1881* (Cambridge: Cambridge University Press, 1995)

Heinz-Dietrich Löwe, *The Tsars and the Jews: Reform, Reaction and Anti-Semitism in Imperial Russia, 1772–1917* (Chur: Harwood, 1993)

Michael A. Meyer (ed.), *German-Jewish History in Modern Times*, vols 2 and 3 (New York: Columbia University Press, 1997)

Peter Pulzer, *Jews and the German State: The Political History of a Minority, 1848–1933* (Oxford: Blackwell, 1992)

David Sorkin, *The Transformation of German Jewry, 1780–1840*
(Oxford: Oxford University Press, 1987)

Michael Stanislawski, *Zionism and the Fin de Siècle: Cosmopolitanism
and Nationalism from Nordau to Jabotinsky* (Berkeley and Los
Angeles: University of California Press, 2001)

4. The culture of irrationalism

Peter Gay, *Freud, Jews and Other Germans: Masters and Victims in
Modernist Culture* (Oxford: Oxford University Press, 1978)

Nancy A. Harrowitz (ed.), *Tainted Greatness: Antisemitism and
Cultural Heroes* (Philadelphia: Temple University Press, 1994)

Jack Jacobs, *On 'The Jewish Question' after Marx* (New York: New
York University Press, 1992)

Jacob Katz, *The Darker Side of Genius: Richard Wagner's
Antisemitism* (Hanover, NH: University Press of New England,
1986)

Michael R. Marrus, *The Politics of Assimilation: The French Jewish
Community at the Time of the Dreyfus Affair* (Oxford: Clarendon
Press, 1971)

William J. McGrath, *Dionysian Art and Populist Politics in Austria*
(New Haven: Yale University Press, 1974)

George L. Mosse, *The Crisis of German Ideology: Intellectual Origins
of the Third Reich* (New York: Schocken, 1981)

Werner E. Mosse, *Jews in the German Economy: The German-Jewish
Economic Elite, 1820–1935* (Oxford: Clarendon Press, 1987)

Michael K. Silber (ed.), *Jews in the Hungarian Economy, 1760–1945*
(Jerusalem: The Magnes Press, 1992)

Fritz Stern, *The Politics of Cultural Despair: A Study in the Rise of
German Ideology* (Berkeley: University of California Press,
1961)

Robert S. Wistrich, *Socialism and the Jews: Dilemmas of Assimilation
in Germany and Austria-Hungary* (London: Associated University
Presses, 1982)

5. The perils of modernity

John W. Boyer, *Political Radicalism in Late Imperial Vienna: Origins
of the Christian Social Movement, 1848–1897* (Chicago: University
of Chicago Press, 1981)

John M. Efron, *Defenders of the Race: Jewish Doctors and Race Science in Fin-de-Siècle Europe* (New Haven: Yale University Press, 1994)

Brigitte Hamann, *Hitler's Vienna: A Dictator's Apprenticeship*, tr. T. Thornton (Oxford: Oxford University Press, 2001)

Nancy A. Harrowitz and Barbara Hyams (eds), *Jews and Gender: Responses to Otto Weininger* (Philadelphia: Temple University Press, 1995)

Jeffrey Herf, *Reactionary Modernism: Technology, Culture and Politics in Weimar and the Third Reich* (Cambridge: Cambridge University Press, 1984)

Pieter M. Judson, *Exclusive Revolutionaries: Liberal Politics, Social Experience and National Identity in the Austrian Empire, 1848–1914* (Ann Arbor: University of Michigan Press, 1996)

Hillel J. Kieval, *The Making of Czech Jewry: National Conflict and Jewish Society in Bohemia, 1870–1918* (Oxford: Oxford University Press, 1988)

Albert S. Lindemann, *The Jew Accused: Three Anti-Semitic Affairs: Dreyfus, Beilis, Frank, 1894–1915* (Cambridge: Cambridge University Press, 1991)

George L. Mosse, *Towards the Final Solution: A History of European Racism* (London: Dent, 1978)

Andrew G. Whiteside, *The Socialism of Fools: Georg Ritter von Schönerer and Austrian Pan-Germanism* (Berkeley: University of California Press, 1975)

6. Concatenations

Steven Beller, *Herzl* (London: Peter Halban, 1991)

Norman Cohn, *Warrant for Genocide: The Myth of the Jewish World-Conspiracy and the Protocols of the Elders of Zion* (London: Serif, 2005)

Harold James, *The German Slump: Politics and Economics, 1924–1936* (Oxford: Clarendon Press, 1986)

Ian Kershaw, *Hitler, 1889–1936: Hubris* (London: Allen Lane, 1998)

Ezra Mendelsohn, *The Jews of East Central Europe Between the World Wars* (Bloomington: Indiana University Press, 1983)

Michael A. Meyer (ed.), *German-Jewish History in Modern Times*, vol. 4 (New York: Columbia University Press, 1998)

Bruce F. Pauley, *From Prejudice to Persecution: A History of Austrian Anti-Semitism* (Chapel Hill: University of North Carolina Press, 1992)

Yuri Slezkine, *The Jewish Century* (Princeton: Princeton University Press, 2004)

7. Consequences

Zygmunt Bauman, *Modernity and the Holocaust* (Ithaca: Cornell University Press, 1989)

Christopher R. Browning, *Ordinary Men: Reserve Battalion 101 and the Final Solution in Poland* (New York: Harper Collins, 1992)

Christopher R. Browning, *The Path to Genocide: Essays on Launching the Final Solution* (Cambridge: Cambridge University Press, 1992)

David Cesarani (ed.), *The Final Solution: Origins and Implementation* (London: Routledge, 1994)

Daniel Jonah Goldhagen, *Hitler's Willing Executioners: Ordinary Germans and the Holocaust* (London: Little, Brown and Co., 1996)

Jan T. Gross, *Neighbors: The Destruction of the Jewish Community in Jedwabne, Poland* (Princeton: Princeton University Press, 2001)

Raul Hilberg, *The Destruction of the European Jews*, 3rd edn, 3 vols (New Haven: Yale University Press, 2003)

Ian Kershaw, *The 'Hitler Myth': Image and Reality in the Third Reich* (Oxford: Clarendon Press, 1987)

Ian Kershaw, *Hitler, 1936–1945: Nemesis* (London: Allen Lane, 2000)

Michael R. Marrus, *The Holocaust in History* (New York: Meridian, 1989)

Ivar Oxaal, Michael Pollak, and Gerhard Botz (eds), *Jews, Antisemitism and Culture in Vienna* (London: Routledge and Kegan Paul, 1987)

Jonathan Steinberg, *All or Nothing: The Axis and the Holocaust, 1941–1943* (London: Routledge, 1990)

8. After Auschwitz

Matti Bunzl, *Symptoms of Modernity: Jews and Queers in Late Twentieth Century Vienna* (Berkeley and Los Angeles: University of California Press, 2004)

David G. Goodman and Masanori Miyazawa, *Jews in the Japanese Mind: The History and Uses of a Cultural Stereotype* (New York: The Free Press, 1995)

Jan T. Gross, *Fear: Anti-Semitism in Poland after Auschwitz: An Essay in Historical Interpretation* (Princeton: Princeton University Press, 2006)

Friedrich Heer, *God's First Love: Christians and Jews over Two Thousand Years* (London: Weidenfeld and Nicolson, 1970)

Tony Judt, *Postwar: A History of Europe since 1945* (London: Penguin Press, 2005)

Tony Kushner, *The Holocaust and the Liberal Imagination: A Social and Cultural History* (Oxford: Blackwell, 1994)

Walter Laqueur, *The Changing Face of Anti-Semitism: From Ancient Times to the Present Day* (Oxford: Oxford University Press, 2006)

Bernard Lewis, *Semites and Anti-Semites: An Inquiry into Conflict and Prejudice*, with a new afterword (New York: Norton, 1999)

Deborah E. Lipstadt, *Denying the Holocaust: The Growing Assault on Truth and Memory* (London: Penguin, 1994)

Douglas Villiers (ed.), *Next Year in Jerusalem: Jews in the Twentieth Century* (London: Harrap, 1976)

Index

Index

Visit the
VERY SHORT INTRODUCTIONS
Web site

www.oup.co.uk/vsi

- ➤ **Information** about all published titles

- ➤ News of **forthcoming books**

- ➤ **Extracts** from the books, including titles not yet published

- ➤ **Reviews** and views

- ➤ **Links** to other **web sites** and main OUP web page

- ➤ Information about **VSIs in translation**

- ➤ **Contact** the editors

- ➤ **Order** other **VSIs** on-line

POLITICS
A Very Short Introduction
Kenneth Minogue

In this provocative but balanced essay, Kenneth Minogue discusses the development of politics from the ancient world to the twentieth century. He prompts us to consider why political systems evolve, how politics offers both power and order in our society, whether democracy is always a good thing, and what future politics may have in the twenty-first century.

> 'This is a fascinating book which sketches, in a very shor space, one view of the nature of politics … the reader is challenged, provoked and stimulated by Minogue's trenchant views.'
> **Ian Davies, *Talking Politics***

> 'a dazzling but unpretentious display of great scholarship and humane reflection'
> **Neil O'Sullivan, University of Hul**

www.oup.co.uk/vsi/politics

HISTORY
A Very Short Introduction
John H. Arnold

History: A Very Short Introduction is a stimulating essay about how we understand the past. The book explores various questions provoked by our understanding of history, and examines how these questions have been answered in the past. Using examples of how historians work, the book shares the sense of excitement at discovering not only the past, but also ourselves.

> 'A stimulating and provocative introduction to one of collective humanity's most important quests – understanding the past and its relation to the present. A vivid mix of telling examples and clear cut analysis.'
>
> **David Lowenthal, University College London**

> 'This is an extremely engaging book, lively, enthusiastic and highly readable, which presents some of the fundamental problems of historical writing in a lucid and accessible manner. As an invitation to the study of history it should be difficult to resist.'
>
> **Peter Burke, Emmanuel College, Cambridge**

www.oup.co.uk/vsi/history

NINETEENTH-CENTURY BRITAIN

A Very Short Introduction

Christopher Harvie & H. C. G. Matthew

First published as part of the best-selling Oxford Illustrated History of Britain, Christopher Harvie and H. C. G. Matthew's Very Short Introduction to nineteenth-century Britain is a sharp but subtle account of remarkable economic and social change – and an even more remarkable political stability. Britain in 1789 was overwhelmingly rural, agrarian, multilingual, and almost half Celtic. By 1914, when it faced its greatest test since the defeat of Napoleon, it was largely urban and English. Christopher Harvie and H. C. G. Matthew show the forces behind Britain's rise to its imperial zenith, and the continuing tensions within the nations and classes of the 'union state'.

www.oup.co.uk/isbn/0-19-285398-8

ISLAM
A Very Short Introduction
Malise Ruthven

Islam features widely in the news, often in its most militant versions, but few people in the non-Muslim world really understand the nature of Islam.

Malise Ruthven's Very Short Introduction contains essential insights into issues such as why Islam has such major divisions between movements such as the Shi'ites, the Sunnis, and the Wahhabis, and the central importance of the Shar'ia (Islamic law) in Islamic life. It also offers fresh perspectives on contemporary questions: Why is the greatest 'Jihad' (holy war) now against the enemies of Islam, rather than the struggle against evil? Can women find fulfilment in Islamic societies? How must Islam adapt as it confronts the modern world?

'Malise Ruthven's book answers the urgent need for an introduction to Islam. ... He addresses major issues with clarity and directness, engages dispassionately with the disparate stereotypes and polemics on the subject, and guides the reader surely through urgent debates about fundamentalism.'

Michael Gilsenan, New York University

www.oup.co.uk/isbn/0-19-285389-9

THE RUSSIAN REVOLUTION

A Very Short Introduction

S. A. Smith

The Bolshevik's aim was nothing less than to destroy an entire social system, and to replace it with one superior to any hitherto seen in human history. In this Very Short Introduction to the Russian Revolution, Steve Smith explores the far-reaching reverberations of the drive to modernize a bakward, isolated Russia. Using the shift in perspective brought about by the fall of Communism and the

such fur Re ving ele Ru ty.

ful and judicious.'

Geoffrey Hosking, University College, London

'Written with verve, this book is a triumph o compression: it will immediately establish itself as the bes short introduction to the subject.'

Simon Dixon, University of Leeds

www.oup.co.uk/isbn/0-19-285395-3